THE CONSERVATION OF CITIES

THE CONSERVATION OF CITIES

UNESCO

ST. MARTIN'S PRESS NEW YORK

THE UNESCO PRESS PARIS

Library of Congress Catalog Card Number: 74–29420
First published in the United States of America in 1975.

The Unesco Press
7 Place de Fontenoy, 75700 Paris
ISBN 92–3–101087–5

AFFILIATED PUBLISHERS: Macmillan Limited, London
—also at Bombay, Calcutta, Madras and Melbourne

CONTENTS

PREFACE

While cities are being re-structured, adapted to movements of population and to the erosion of buildings, it is time to give more attention to values other than those of the necessary new functional architecture.

The centripetal attraction of cities has been notably evident in the years since World War II. The gregariousness of humankind has of course been clearly seen since tribal agglomerations formed cities some eight thousand years ago. On every continent, today, masses of people grouped in cities are growing, assembled not only by necessity but by choice. Obviously, many millions like to be in cities — for city life is not necessarily a hardship, it can give satisfaction and comfort.

A question today is whether some of the great efforts being carried on for cities are leading towards improvement or deterioration of the quality of life. The rapidity sought in adapting resources to growing numbers has sometimes involved inadequate planning — to judge by the complaints heard in numerous communities where citizens have protested against losses of the quality of their days. There are outcries demanding conservation — the rescue or restoration of even such essentials as fresh air to replace a polluted kind, of trees, of natural vistas — and for the saving of structures which have visual, historic, or inspirational attributes.

The need of conservation can apply not only to a favourite little park or bank of a stream in one's home city but also to modest monuments that recall merely local events or personages of just this century or the last — for local pride is a pleasing sentiment. The monuments of world fame which remind mankind of its most momentous events should not be the only objects of conservation. There is a relationship between the salvage of a great relic of antiquity, far away, and the saving of only locally known notable features of one's own home city. The ideal of conservation carried on afar can inspire peoples everywhere to look at historical values of their own cities and to treasure them, to increase the enjoyment of their own days.

This book represents reactions, with emphasis in the cause of conservation, to some of the changes occurring in cities around the world, as well as recognition of the necessity of large-scale change. And it provides a record of much valiant effort being carried on for the adaptation of old places to new conditions, and for conservation, and it offers some opinion on problems involved.

7

Unesco is active in the cause of historic conservation in various parts of the world. A detailed list of its activities and missions will be found in Appendix I.

The views expressed by the writers in this book are not necessarily those of Unesco. To the authors and to those who contributed illustrations Unesco expresses its appreciation.

INTRODUCTION: URBAN RETRIEVAL TOO

Hiroshi Daifuku

Changes in the urban environment have been taking place with vertiginous speed in major cities throughout the world. Their growth has outstripped the predictions made by planners, architects and social scientists. Many cities which had populations of a few hundred thousand twenty years ago now have become cities of a million or more. The greater ones have grown enormously, engulfing nearby towns, villages and municipalities and at times coalescing into large conglomerations forming megalopolises.

At an earlier stage in their growth cities were located in fertile plains, along rivers, lakes, harbours where food production was assured and commerce was easy for the means of transportation at hand. Their unchecked growth has resulted in once fertile fields being covered with cement and asphalt, in polluted rivers and streams, coastlines of lakes and seas, and if continued not only threatens the balance of nature but eventually the production of food upon which all civilisation is based. While the average standard of living throughout the world, even among the poorer countries, is much higher than it was a few decades ago, yet there are already signs that growth will not continue unchecked. The recent petroleum crisis is but an indication that the resources of the world are finite. Discontent and dissatisfaction with material progress are all too prevalent and such discontent is frequently found among urban populations.

Cities have been the foci of social development over the ages. If there are problems which menace their survival or their role of contributing to the growth of civilisation, these ills must be studied, understood, and eventually measures taken to ensure continued urban health. A great deal of study has been devoted to ecological relations in the biosphere. However, studies of comparative depth using multi-disciplinary analyses of the urban environment have still to be undertaken. The fact that the introduction of new elements results in profound changes in environmental relationships among the different species composing the biosphere has been long accepted as a truism.

Cities also have environmental relationships but they are less understood because they are still, on the whole, largely unacknowledged and unidentified. Changes and modifications are still planned and carried out without considering cities holistically. The effects of such changes are frequently less favourable than when first considered due to this lack.

Many of the ills which plague urban development today are based upon 'common sense' programmes thought of and begun several decades ago. The rapid development of the physical sciences and technology seemed to many to promise the means for recovery from the economic depression of the 1930s and from the effects of World War II. This faith affected not only the expansion of industry, the design of new and more efficient machinery, but also designs for living. 'Functional' standards prevailed as buildings and furniture were thought of in terms of 'machines' for living. Inevitably it became fashionable to scorn the elaborate façades characteristic of earlier architectural styles (Baroque, Victorian, Gothic in the West and the traditional architectural forms of other civilisations). Stark cubical forms, the use of metals and eventually plastics in place of traditional materials have marked architectural design of the past few decades.

The rapid growth of the world's economy has contributed to the well-being of many and as a result the average standard of living is higher today for most of the people of the world. Mass production has placed at the disposal of large groups of people articles which were once the prerogative of the wealthy.

Of these products the automobile has been, perhaps, the most pervasive and has had profound effects on the urban environment. Within cities the sight of masses of cars creeping along through crowded streets have become banal, even among cities found in countries undergoing rapid development. The fumes of their motors affect the atmosphere of cities so that they have a pall of partially oxidised hydrocarbons, nitrous fumes, and other products such as lead (from gasoline), powdered synthetics worn from tyres, etc. Trees which once lined streets or highways die and need frequent replacement or else are sacrificed in order to widen streets and thoroughfares for even more cars and for additional space for them to park.

The use of the motor car has contributed to the decay of the cities' cores as many people flee to the suburbs. It has affected the family, for men commuting to work leave children with their mothers for most of the day resulting in matrilocal and matriarchal patterns of living in contrast to older patterns when the husband and father lived in or nearby his place of work. If both spouses commute then the suburban home remains untenanted during the day and contributes to the pattern of 'dormitory' towns existing as satellites to the city.

Physical changes take place as streets are widened, or else become uninviting as the superabundance of cars lead to their being parked on side walks or on curbs. As street life disappears, in part from the pressure of the car, modern cities present a bleak and at times hostile atmosphere at night after the cars and their owners depart. In efforts to reverse this trend, the concept known as 'urban renewal' has guided efforts to rebuild or redesign the interior of cities to accommodate them to the use of the car and to the change in residence patterns it has helped to introduce. Two hypotheses seem to guide such programmes: first, the need to improve accessibility for cars (widen streets, provide parking, improve access routes to the city, etc.); second, to destroy older buildings and replace them with high-rise structures so as to: *a)* provide modern accommodations for commerce or for residences; *b)* permit greater (vertical) density of population where the cost of urban real estate is high; and *c)* produce greater income for the city. These premises are based upon optimistic, and perhaps mechanistic, solutions to provide a healthy environment for urban residents.

'Renewal' implies hope and cheer but it has a negative aspect too, the removal of the old to make way for the new. In practice this has meant not only the elimination of decay, the cutting out of lesions and abscesses in the urban body, but also quite radical surgery. In reaction private groups, such as committees to preserve the former mansions surrounding Park Monceau in Paris, or the historic city of Bamberg in the Federal Republic of Germany, or of Bath in England, have been formed. Such groups, at times supported by the press, are another indication that achievements in urban renewal have not kept pace with promise and that many of the fondest hopes of the planners and leading experts in the field have demonstrated an over-confident approach towards the ills that plague industrialised urban society. Urban renewal projects based on the use of land plans, street maps, statistical tables, seem to show that all too many have been prepared by specialists who have been narrowly bound by their training without awareness of the overall consequences. It was assumed *a priori*, for example, that certain areas were decaying and contributing to the malaise of a city. Perhaps these localities contained old residences since converted into shops or rooming houses, old warehouses, or well-worn buildings of outmoded industries. However, recent studies have shown that many such old and worn quarters of a city — just as marshlands fronting a sea — may have an important functional role in urban ecology. It is in such areas that shops selling worn, but still useful machinery, old books and furniture (not high priced antiques but items useful to the urban poor or to newly married couples) can be bought and sold. Frequently, many large successful industries had their beginnings in such low rent, humble surroundings. Older residential quarters also serve as a transitional zone for immigrants coming into the city from the countryside or from abroad. In time such neighbourhoods may find new life, as the people develop a strong sense of identification and cooperation and form a community.

The notion of renewal should be broadened to mean also 'urban retrieval', for what is valuable of the old should be kept. Radical change may cause more harm to cities than a more careful and restrained treatment. Rescue and restoration, the revitalisation of what had once been vigorous and living quarters of the city – the actions signified by the verb 'retrieve' – can contribute towards the salvage of the quality of the urban environment.

Loss of Traditional Skills

It was not until early man first domesticated plants and animals, permitting an economic base which was not devoted exclusively to the production and the consumption of food, that it was possible to have large social units. In turn this enabled the development of various types of occupations which were not immediately concerned with food production and the rise of urban civilisations. This change took place gradually in many places of the world, in ancient Egypt and Mesopotamia, in the Indus Valley, in the Yangtze, and in Middle America and the central Andes. In time the socio-economic and political lessons learned were diffused and gave rise to other urban civilisations. Each gave rise to individual solutions underlying the diversity of past civilisations. The massive walls of the fortress of Sacsahuaman, built by the Incas, were for defence as well as to impress potential foes with the might of the Inca state and its organisation . . . the lines of fortresses and walls erected by Hadrian in Britain, the Great Wall built by the Ch'in emperors in China were erected for similar reasons. Motives of piety and of pride underlay the construction of the Parthenon in Athens, of the major Gothic cathedrals of Europe, and of the great temples of the sun and of the moon erected in the Valley of Mexico by the Toltecs. These great monuments survive and are cherished today as examples of the achievements, the hopes and fears, of past generations.

Cities too have their own history and tradition. Like the cultures of which they are part, they live or die. The generations which inhabited cities contributed to their development. At the turn of the century, when industrialisation was still in its infancy, each city was characterised by the work of its craftsmen and artisans. Their skills represented the accumulated experience of generations which were modified due to historical and geographical influence. Thus variations were constant. Within a city a given quarter would have houses which reflected the social and economic status of the neighbourhood or the prevailing styles of a given period. The varied city-scape, provided a rhythm which formed vivid backgrounds to the life in the streets, squares, canals or parks, etc. Once destroyed they will not be replaced (except under very exceptional circumstances) as the skills required are lost or have become prohibitively expensive to recruit.

Mass Production and the High-rise Building

The early industrial revolution was not without its depressed and squalid areas of habitation. Sweat shops, child labour, long working hours underlay the origins of this period. Similar conditions still prevail in many countries undergoing rapid development. No one will deny the benefits which have since resulted with greater perfection of machines and the resultant low unit cost of materials which have been produced. The hope of many, living in countries undergoing rapid development, lies in the transition to industrialised economies and the gains to be gotten from mass production.

Nevertheless there is a negative aspect to the gain. The flood of goods which is being produced is based on the principle of using a limited range of designs so that material can be produced by machinery with a minimal amount of labour and, ideally, with a minimal amount of maintenance.

This has had a tremendous impact on architectural design. As in other trades artisans and craftsmen have been disappearing rapidly. The long apprenticeship which was once required for the acquisition of skills runs counter to current trends. The architect therefore is forced to find most of the components used in buildings from catalogues produced by major manufacturers. For the most part he chooses items which are in stock due to reasons of price and availability. Special runs of products which are not part of the regular stock may be carried out for large projects — within the limitations of the machinery in use but anything out of the ordinary still requires hand craftsmanship. The current trend to use 'curtain wall' construction (using external panels made of glass, metal, or composition in factories) speeds construction, lessens costs, but adds to the monotony of the contemporary urban scene.

Manhattan Island, New York City is the outstanding example of the use of high-rise structures, and impressive rows of skyscrapers form its famed skyline. Within the confines of the island, long the financial capital and chief sea port of the United States, the high cost of urban real estate led to the early development of high-rise structures. The bedrock, of good quality granite, is close to the surface and forms a solid foundation for these towering buildings. To many, the high-rise building has become the symbol of twentieth-century architecture and represents the successful attainment of an industrialised economy. They are being built everywhere, even among the non-industrialised countries where nearly all of the materials used have to be imported at considerable cost. As a result newer quarters of cities which are culturally and geographically distant — such as Tokyo, Japan; Bangkok, Thailand; Dakar, Senegal; Brussels, Belgium; San Francisco, California — resemble

A view of Grenoble

each other more than they do their own older quarters.

The continued construction of high-rise buildings is not due entirely to faddism and status seeking. For many years leading town planning experts and architects have recommended the high-rise as the answer to problems of urban growth and the necessity to adapt the city to contemporary requirements. It was argued that their construction would attract large enterprises, re-vitalise decaying centres and make best use of expensive urban real estate.

In the United States, 'where it all began', a series of studies was carried out in the city of San Francisco, California — once renowned as one of the most attractive in the country. It has embarked on a programme to become a second Manhattan and the leading commercial and financial centre of the United States in the Pacific. It now has one of the highest percentages of high-rise structures of any American city. The consequences were carefully evaluated in a series of studies undertaken by economists, social scientists, journalists, etc. The results were published by the *San Francisco Bay Guardian* in a book edited by B. Brugmann and G. Sletteland, *The Ultimate Highrise: San Francisco's Mad Rush Toward the Sky* (1971). The results were enlightening:

a) the commercial high-rise centre contributed in forms of taxes $5 million less than it cost the city for services;

b) real estate tax payments declined by 16 per cent as a proportion of the total amount paid to the city over the past decade;

c) new tax assessments, based upon high density occupation of the areas where high-rise structures were erected increased assessments in neighbouring areas as much as 380 per cent leading frequently to the destruction of the character of the neighbourhood;

d) changing patterns of land use resulted in over 100,000 middle income San Franciscans migrating to the suburbs;

e) in terms of employment a few salaried posts were created, but over 14,000 semi-skilled workers lost their employment and tripled the welfare rolls of the city;

f) new mass transportation facilities which were required are estimated to cost over $5 billion during a ten-year period;

g) police costs are ten times higher in high-rise districts than elsewhere in the city;

h) the added pollution will cost the city nearly $1 billion to clean up (pp.31-2 *ibid.*)

The experience of San Francisco is not unique. Everywhere in the world where decisions have been taken to permit the massive introduction of high-rise structures, the ecology of the city has changed. The new and improved services required in the way of investments, such as building new plants for the production of electricity. (It might be

Maine – Montparnasse Tower, Paris

noted that high-rise structures can function only with a dependable supply of electricity for its lifts, air-conditioning plants, lighting, etc. — not always available in cities in countries undergoing rapid development. Recent 'brown-outs' in New York City have resulted in the sight of people living or working in high-rise structures suffering from the heat or laboriously using stairs.) Streets need to be widened to adjust to the increased density of the population, mass transportation improved, etc. In turn these investments, in order to be amortised, result in further construction of high-rise structures. Like cancerous growths they seem to create their own environment, favourable to their expansion at the expense of the rest of the city.

Analogous changes are now taking place in the city of Paris. Regulations were once strictly enforced controlling the height of buildings so that they did not top the Arc de Triomphe. In practice buildings were usually eight to ten stories in height. New construction while not uncommon, was limited to the slow removal of lower buildings and their replacement by others within this limitation. In the 1950s it was still possible for the critic Lewis Mumford to remark that of all the great cities of the world Paris still kept its human scale. High-rise structures were first permitted in the Defense area, a suburb north of Paris. Great office blocks were raised, highways improved resulting in the 'concrete spaghetti' of over-passes, under-passes, and throughways; in addition a new special high-speed subway linking the Defense area with Paris and the Western suburbs has been constructed. When it was decided to build a new railroad station at Montparnasse, consolidating the older one with the Maine station, not only were new office blocks permitted but also a skyscraper of over sixty stories. The Montparnasse Tower now dominates the southern skyline (once the sole prerogative of the Eiffel Tower), around it new over- and under-passes have been built, new shops, etc. The neighbourhood, still a haunt of artists, small art supply stores, restaurants, is gradually changing its character. Elsewhere in the city, except for a few *arrondissements*, other high-rise structures are rising and the skyline admired by so many, is fast acquiring the appearance of a typical twentieth-century large city.

Handicaps of Massive Construction

It is now recognised by some town planners and architects that large 'new towns' or huge blocks of buildings and towered structures with identical or nearly identical buildings, interspersed with a few shopping centres, have proved far from adequate for their professed purpose to improve the lives of their inhabitants. People living in such areas where the buildings and their surroundings are but a few years old, gradually lose a sense of time and become ahistorical as they have no visual reference to remind them of the continuity of their civilisation and of the mores which have shaped it. The buildings dominate the surroundings, imposing their bulk upon the people. 'Anomie', the loss of identification and of mores, becomes a common ill. The sense of detachment and resultant loss of group responsibility contributes to the loss of standards and eventually to the growth of crime.

In the United States where urban renewal has taken place at the most rapid rate, dissatisfaction with much of the results obtained have been quite widespread. A number of leading critics have reviewed the programme including the effects of displacement and resettlement on the original inhabitants of an area which has been 'renewed'. Thus for example, Marc Fried in a study 'Grieving for a Lost Home; psychological costs of relocation' (published in *Urban Renewal: the record and the controversy*, MIT Press, 1966) reported that:

'the post-relocation experiences of a great many people have borne out their most pessimistic pre-location expectations . . . for the majority it seems quite precise to speak of their reactions as expressions of *grief*. These are manifest in the feelings of painful loss, the continued longing, the general depressive tone, frequent symptoms of psychological or social or semantic distress . . .' (p.359).

Foramitti and Piperek found data in their Vienna studies indicating similar effects.

Urban Retrieval

The problem of choice between 'renewal' and 'retrieval' can be dramatic. During World War II the centres of both Rotterdam and Warsaw were destroyed. In the case of the former a great deal of discussion took place as to whether to attempt to rebuild the centre of the city in traditional architectural styles or to introduce new construction. In view of the near total destruction it was decided by the authorities concerned to rebuild central Rotterdam in contemporary design. On the other hand, the old centre of Warsaw, which was also systematically destroyed, was considered to be so important for the need to have continuity in tradition and to establish a sense of identification for the city as the ancient capital of the country that great pains were taken to ensure that the old centre of the city would regain its former appearance. Architectural drawings which had been prepared by students for training in the pre-war days were used together with scenes of Warsaw painted by Bernardo Bellotto (also

18

known as 'Canaletto the Younger') during the eighteenth century to establish building plans and the project was carried out and completed at considerable cost.

In many other cities where a great deal of destruction has taken place or where urban expansion has introduced pressures to renew similar decisions have been taken — at times to rebuild or to reconstruct ancient buildings of historic importance, at others to replace them by completely new structures. In Paris, in contrast to the decisions permitting the construction of the Montparnasse Tower and the massive new buildings along the Left Bank in the 15th (south-western) *arrondissement* retrieval or renovation is taking place in the Marais district of the older part of the city.

As the need for concerted action grew, not only have projects for conservation been planned on a national scale but many regional as well as international organisations have taken up the problem. Among these are the Cultural Council of the Council of Europe which has sponsored a series of studies on the preservation of historic quarters and cities; such non-governmental organisations as ICOMOS (the International Council of Monuments and Sites); IFHP (International Federation of Housing and Planning); IFLA (International Federation of Landscape Architects; IUA (International Union of Architects), etc. They serve, not only to stimulate research and the interchange of information, but also help in encouraging national administrative and legislative measures required.

Programmes of technical aid have expanded continually over the course of the years as they have reflected the real needs of many states, and there has been a widening scope for the work of experts. Newly independent states which were at first sensitive about their ex-colonial status have sought later to find in their remote past historical justification for their national groupings. And, with time, new states have considered it wise to save buildings of the colonial period, as structures of historic value. For example many countries in Africa have endeavoured to maintain or restore buildings erected during the period when they were colonies under European domination as part of a movement to preserve their history and traditions which form their contemporary societies. In Ghana fortifications have been restored, well-maintained and used as museums or as official buildings. In Senegal plans are under way for the preservation of the Gorée and St Louis islands not far from Dakar.

Tourism Aiding National Economies

The potential importance of sites and monuments, and of historic cities that keep their evidence of history, for the development of

national economies through tourism, was recognised by the United
Nations Development Programme (UNDP). It is now possible for
Unesco to aid many of its Member States under this programme.
Experts have been recruited for such projects, and they include architect-
restorers, town planners and specialists in terrestrial photogrammetry.
In many cities it is now recognised that the preservation of an historic
quarter implies not only the safeguarding of a useful urban environment,
but also a potential stimulus to tourism. The development banks, such
as the World Bank (IBRD) and the Inter-American Development Bank
(IDB) also finance cultural tourism projects in collaboration
with Unesco.

Tourism based in history is a motivating factor for projects in
various parts of the world. In Kyoto, a city in a country that suffered
devastation by war, and in an area of recent industrial development,
public interest and support for the preservation of the historic aspects
of the city have been aroused by a Unesco-sponsored symposium. In
similar projects elsewhere the preservation of the historic quality of the
city plays an important economic, social and cultural role. Another is
the project of the Government of Peru to preserve ancient Inca
monuments for which experts are being furnished by Unesco under the
UNDP. Together with this a town planning and urban retrieval project
is under way for the ancient Inca and Spanish Colonial capital of
Cuzco. The living conditions of the people are to be improved and new
employment outlets are being planned for an area which has been
economically depressed for many years. Other projects for which
experts have been furnished under Unesco/UNDP include the
preservation and development of the historic cities of Isfahan in Iran;
the Medina of Tunis in Tunisia; Ouro Preto in Brazil, etc. In each case
part of the costs of the investments required will be amortised through
the development of tourism.

One of the most spectacular projects for the conservation of
cultural property undertaken by Unesco was the campaign to preserve
the rock-cut temples of Abu-Simbel in Upper Egypt. The experience
gained in obtaining the support of the international community in
carrying out the project to its successful completion, was undoubtedly
a factor contributing to the role Unesco now has for the project to
safeguard the historic city of Venice.

The General Conference of Unesco happened to be in session when
the great 1966 floods struck Florence and a combination of factors
led to the inundation of Venice. It was immediately decided to respond
to the appeal for aid. Equipment was furnished and eventually much of
the assistance given was channelled through Unesco. During the first
year of conservation and restoration, priority was given to the need to
preserve the delicate and irreplaceable works of art which were damaged

Nubia: Island of Philae

by water, pollutants, etc., in the City of Florence.

It became evident that long-term works, possible only through the support of the international community, were needed to save Venice. Unesco contributed towards studies which were carried out by scientists from the International Centre for the Study of the Preservation and the restoration of Cultural Property (the 'Rome Centre') of air pollution and capillary action on the buildings and cultural property in Venice. Other contracts were made to carry out studies of the lagoon and factors leading to the so-called 'high-water' phenomena: the problem of currents and of marine pollution were investigated as well as the problem of the lowering of the water-table due to the use of artesian wells, etc. The human factor was not neglected in the studies. A detailed sociological examination was carried out to determine the present and future needs of the residents of Venice. The summary of this report is included in Chapter 9 as many of the problems experienced in Venice of living in ancient housing, which requires measures to rehabilitate it for contemporary use furnish lessons for other cities.

On the basis of these studies and recommendations of an international Committee of Consultants established by the Government of Italy, legislation was enacted and adopted which would enable the Government to float loans of more than $500 million to undertake the work required so that Venice can be saved. Internationally certain palaces and other structures were individually 'adopted' by governmental and private organisations for restoration. Several of the most noted Venetian churches are today recovering from the ravages of time and weather through such assistance. The response of peoples from various parts of the world to the call to save old Venice encouraged the Italian Government to plan the solution of more basic problems; to eliminate natural and man-made menaces to the survival of the city. When finally carried out, with the resources which have been promised, Venice will become an outstanding example of the rescue of an historic city, a rescue which will have repercussions on the economy of the region, and on the social and cultural heritage of the people of Italy.

The problems of contemporary cities are manifold and the results of urban renewal programmes have not always lived up to their promises. The situation has become so critical that some leading architects have proposed the construction of new 'villages' within major cities — areas where buildings will be low, where there will be green space, and where the residents will form a stable nucleus within the metropolis. It is probable that after a period of time, given a favourable environment, stable communities will form there. It is also probable that in view of the costs, in particular of urban real estate in newly built areas, these villages will be largely composed of residents from the

22

middle and upper-middle classes. It would seem less expensive and indeed more practical to ensure the survival of older residential and commercial quarters within the city. They would have the advantage already of having stable groups which formed over a period of time, and moreover be much more heterogenous in age and class structure so that true interdependence of functions would exist.

In many cases, as noted in the study of San Francisco, a neighbourhood worth saving need not be particularly distinguished or artistically or historically important. Nevertheless its saving maintains the traditional ambiance of the city whose buildings therefore continue to be more human in scale. Because of the varied architecture styles they continue to contribute to the visual rhythm of the cityscape which would otherwise be lost. The reasons for ensuring the survival of an historic quarter or city are even more cogent. For with their destruction, a page, a chapter, of the life of the city and of the history of urban civilisation would be irremediably lost.

1. WHY TROUBLE WITH HISTORIC TOWNS?

Graeme Shankland

This question has to be put because the first sharp lesson learned
by anyone who has worked on historic towns is that their conservation
takes a disproportionate amount of time, money and administrative
and political negotiation as compared with that normally demanded
by administration, planning and building. It is quicker, politically more
dramatic, and often cheaper to bulldoze, or build on open fields.

Very clear justification is necessary, particularly in developing
countries where available resources are usually scarcer, and the scramble
for development on almost any terms tends to sweep all other
considerations aside.

It is striking, however, that, despite the obvious economic
disadvantages, historic conservation claims a high place in the
priorities of nations of very different political outlook, and sometimes
in surprising circumstances. The Soviet Union and Spain both spend a
lot on conservation. Poland re-erected the statue to King Sigismund
when many citizens of its capital were still living in caves, and Warsaw
now intends to rebuild a replica of the Royal Palace that was destroyed.
The newer countries of the Americas and Africa may spend less
because they have less of this particular kind of heritage to conserve.
But they may value what they have even more. Australia's urban
heritage from the nineteenth century is all the more appreciated as it is
increasingly threatened by re-development.

Countries with little architectural heritage have, in a way, to invent
their past. But in another sense, each generation in any country
rediscovers the past, and the values it places on its artistic heritage may
be different from those of previous generations. Newly-independent
countries in the Caribbean, whose early culture and history were
emptied into the dustbin of slavery, are now beginning to spend money
on conserving the former homes of the slave-owners. In Sydney — one
of the booming, *laissez-faire* cities of the world — a popular
conservation movement succeeded in preventing the destruction of
whole areas of pleasant nineteenth-century terrace housing threatened
by new public highway projects; and its latest and smartest restaurant
and night club, with a band dressed in convict clothes, shares a
converted bonded warehouse with an arts centre.

A clear economic case can sometimes be made for the conservation
of streets, or even of towns, particularly if the tourist potential is
strong, and home and foreign visitors are a growing source of income

and economic support. In many smaller and poorer countries, tourist development represents the main hope of economic improvement and social development. (It should be less environmentally destructive than certain sudden discoveries like that of bauxite or oil.) Even Venice's survival depends to some extent on what tourists remember of it, and on the extent to which Italian and world opinion is consequently prepared to pay out hard cash.

I believe, however, that the desire and determination to maintain the fabric of historic towns, villages and buildings draws on very deep psychic sources in national consciousness, and on psycho-social forces in a nation's culture that are only partly conscious. When France and Poland embark on costly policies of restoring and cleaning streets and monuments, for instance, it is such sources that are being tapped.

This almost magical power of the past does not lie only in the intrinsic beauty of what is being preserved, survivals of an age when towns were made by artisans, but above all in the identity they confer. This sense of continuity seems today more important than ever, as national groups and ethnic minorities battle for identity and survival in an age of multi-national economic groupings, uniform machine-made products, and supra-national political settlements.

Historic towns and buildings offer this link. They are distinguishable, one town from another, at a time when new urban development is increasingly standardised and de-personalised. A town without old buildings has less character. This lack of personality is one of the problems of new towns.

Psychologists lay great stress on the importance of identity to individuals and groups as something they must maintain in the face of social and economic developments that offer physical comfort, security and cheaper products at the price of de-personalisation.

For, in any country, what distinguishes one town or city from another is its surroundings, its design and its history. Most other features will be common. Towns of similar size will have comparable services; one mining village will resemble another, and so will commuter suburbs.

The influence of history is different. Towns, parts of towns, streets, even individual houses may bear a particular historical stamp. Towns which have developed in stages over the years, as have most of those we admire in Britain, for example, constitute a unique open museum of diverse architectural forms. Even if the styles of building are the same, they are not assembled on the same street in the same sequence; and they both embody the skill of their individual designers and makers, and the decisions and the idiosyncrasies of successive town authorities.

To any generation, an identifiable past offers a line of communication with others: between the living, the dead, and those still to be born. It provides a reference to previous experience; an illustration of how

The East Gate at Chester, England

men went about creating a civilised environment; a reservoir and perpetual source of historical delight; a culture to be accepted, altered, rejected, re-interpreted or rediscovered.

A country without a past has the emptiness of a barren continent; and a city without old buildings is like a man without a memory.

The Threat to Historic Towns

Many historic towns have been conserved largely by accident. In future they will most likely be conserved by deliberate decision or not at all.

The sacking of cities was normal practice in earlier warfare. Nevertheless, despite slaughter and arson, much of the fabric of towns survived (except when they were made of wood and burned easily, as happened in the case of many Japanese and mediaeval European cities). Towns have been destroyed during the last hundred years by high explosives. Some have been rebuilt almost exactly as they were (Leningrad, Warsaw and Dresden are recent examples).

Today, the biggest and most usual threat comes from random demands imposed by modern life: population pressures, increased prosperity, public services, private speculation and, above all, the motor vehicle. Most of the pressures for change are generated within the town itself. New families need homes and jobs. They expect a higher standard of life than their parents enjoyed — higher wages, better homes, public services at their doorstep.

These demands are a main cause of migration to towns, where the population builds up. But even if such services can be provided in villages, or are not needed, staying in a village means accepting traditional village life, its customs and standards, and limited job opportunities — the very things many young people are no longer prepared to accept.

Paradoxically enough, it is often more expensive in terms of capital cost to provide such services in cities than it is in smaller towns which can operate quite satisfactorily with, for example, septic tank sewage disposal works. Apart from roads, sewage disposal is normally the biggest item in urban capital equipment. It can be very destructive of the mediaeval urban fabric and of the streets and buildings. As it requires a large capital outlay, villages are unlikely to be the beneficiaries. But while the cost may be greater in cities, the money is more likely to be available.

A fresh water supply can usually be piped comparatively easily, but the disposal of water and human wastes demands large diameter pipes and complex main drainage networks which are difficult to introduce into old towns.

27

Electricity is the most flexible and cheapest to install of all modernising services. Unlike drainage, high tension cables can be most cheaply installed overground; to bury them costs several times the price of installation along a public highway. Cables are rarely buried in places where development is rapid, even in countries which could afford it.

Hence the wires and poles or pylons which litter so many historic towns. Delegates to a conservation conference organised by the Japanese National Commission for Unesco and held in Kyoto and Nara in 1970 will recall Professor Kaizuka saying, as he looked along one beautiful street which he loved, 'Nothing has changed here since my boyhood'. When it was gently pointed out to him that he was standing in front of a ten-metre reinforced concrete pylon supporting a network of wires, he replied with a smile, 'Ah, we Japanese have learned to swallow reinforced concrete'.

It will prove difficult to regurgitate. Unfortunately the gradual introduction of unsightly features passes unnoticed by the inhabitants; it is the visitor or the returning inhabitant who sees, with fresh eyes, what has happened. Along the Italian Riviera, the sea near the beaches is often polluted by untreated sewage effluent. Plant could have been installed cheaply seventy years ago — as it was in other countries — when seaside resorts were becoming popular. Now it may never be done, or done at enormously increased cost.

But in advanced countries, it is the motor vehicle (mobile home and portable personal territory) — first major purchase after a man has secured the basic essentials — that today represents the biggest threat to historic towns. Once bought, a car must be used continually and everywhere. It takes up half the floor area of a small house, invades streets, pavements, squares, gardens. The lodger welcomed for a short stay wants to become a member of the family. Can it be domesticated?

There is a good deal of humbug in the pious but powerless injunctions used about conservation and the environment. Is it feasible to force the owner of a building to conserve or renovate it if he has not the means to do so? Britain has a powerful conservation movement, and thousands of local societies are dedicated to opposing undesirable change in their communities. They are usually very vocal, but their protests are not matched by the conservation resources they or anyone else can command. Conservation projects can degenerate into fruitless talking unless (as is generally the case in Eastern Europe), adequate public funds are made available.

Conservation movements in Britain and Western Europe tend to be sincere, dedicated and middle-class, if not positively aristocratic. To resist change becomes a public duty. But this may impose unequal or unjust burdens, and the social and economic implications must always be thoroughly thought out beforehand.

This of course is not to deny the immense educational value of conservation movements. They extend awareness of the individual, local and national heritage, the need to care for buildings, spaces and landscapes. They raise a community's sights and standards, and eventually secure public backing and resources. But the aims should never be wholly unrealistic, or they will be discredited; they must be economically and socially feasible.

Conservation: National and Local

Comparatively little can be done by private initiative alone. Larger conservation measures require governmental and public action.

Objectives can be considered under three main headings: national, regional, and local.

The government must decide what legislation is needed to protect historic towns and buildings; what interdepartmental co-ordination is necessary to ensure that conservation is not frustrated by highway authorities and other public bodies; what funds can be provided to preserve private buildings; what expert services can be provided to schedule historic buildings, supervise conservation, and advise on the technical aspects of restoration and similar matters. The effectiveness of government action will for better or worse determine the effectiveness of national urban planning and land use. Fiscal and tax arrangements can be used to facilitate or encourage particular forms of conservation.

Social and economic development may sometimes conflict with conservation schemes. An engineer and planner from Damascus, deeply concerned with cultural values and asked to devise a practical plan to conserve the old city of Damascus, put the dilemma this way: 'I am under attack from both sides. The archaeologists do not want anything touched and everything restored; the revolutionaries want to sweep away everything that is old as it impedes social progress and modernisation.'

Governments will often have to intervene with policy directives to solve such dilemmas. In Britain, for instance, the Minister for the Environment can decide specific conservation issues, overruling local authorities if need be, and he can adjudicate on the merits of particular plans and alternative planning proposals. British conservationists usually complain that these powers are not used enough. This is certainly my view. They do, however, exist, although their invocation often depends more upon the nuisance value of local protest than the sensitivity of ministries and their ministerial advisers.

A government may inaugurate specific programmes, selecting certain historic towns for special treatment (as in France), rebuilding former palaces (as in the Soviet Union), launching a project that requires international support (campaign of the Government of the Arab Republic of Egypt in conjunction with Unesco to save Abu Simbel and the Nubian temples).

In general, the action or inaction of a government will set the tone and tempo of a nation's conservation. It will be influenced by public opinion which in many countries is increasingly interested, and tends to be restive and critical of 'too little and too late' policies.

It is in regions or other large local government areas that many of the key decisions can and will be taken. In this sense, large cities constitute regions. These decisions affect the appearance of our towns, the quality and extent of their public services, and the allocation of funds for the conservation of historic quarters.

In most countries, it is rare for the government to overrule a city on a large conservation or planning issue. York, one of the most important historic cities in England, with a poor conservation record, received a carefully thought-out conservation plan commissioned by the Government, but refused to implement it, and the Government has not taken any effective action to make it do so. It is sad and puzzling that the municipal authorities of such historic towns as York, Edinburgh and Bristol have bad records in conservation and planning as compared with other cities which are much less worth conserving.

The detailed control of development is regional or local, *e.g.* the detailed design of roads, the adoption of by-laws, the supervision of building, health and amenities. No conservation plan can be carried through without the support of the local authorities concerned; their officials enforce specific conservation measures and deal with the supervision and approval of plans. National legislation usually governs incentives and grants offered to private owners, but the actual administration is probably local.

It is locally that public reactions are most sensitive and can best be tested. If informed local opinion does not continuously press for conservation, either little will be done or what is done will be of poor quality.

Plans and Policies

The preparation of conservation plans falls into two stages: a first stage of studying all the relevant factors and points of view, and a second, detailed planning stage.

Sometimes it is impossible, for the time being at least, to get beyond the first stage. For instance, developing countries cannot find the necessary funds, or can only accord a low priority to conservation; or a report prepared by consultants after visits lasting two to four weeks permits a preliminary assessment and suggestions only.

The purpose of the first stage is to identify and define the problems and opportunities clearly. What does this involve?

The overriding objective – the preservation of the existing quality of a place – must be reconciled with changes, some of them inevitable. If the historic fabric (buildings, streets, open spaces, monuments) can be maintained only by improvements, repairs and adaptation, it may paradoxically be necessary to change the function, uses and social status of buildings, streets and districts in order to secure the necessary funds. Public subsidy may be needed to keep rents low and ensure maintenance.

Several points have to be considered. Firstly, is conservation feasible in physical and financial terms? Secondly, what area is to be conserved? Thirdly, what relation does this area bear to the rest of the town, or to the landscape (in the case of a small town or village). Towns like Isfahan or Venice constitute special cases which will be dealt with later.

Very often in Europe, one part of an old city – perhaps its centre – is surrounded by more modern sectors and is subject to pressure within and without as the city continues to expand. Physical factors and socio-economic forces are involved.

To examine the physical factors, an analysis of constraints and possibilities is prepared: an analysis of topography, fixed factors, the area to be conserved, land available for building, possible re-development areas, development areas too new or valuable for alteration to be feasible, roads, rail and other communications. Towns have natural boundaries with the surrounding landscape. This examination of the main physical features of the town will show the potential locations of future growth.

Socio-economic projections are simultaneously made of the likely minimum and maximum growth of population and employment, to find out how much land and floor space is needed for all purposes. The likely redevelopment can then be worked out, including traffic pressures from private and public transport.

This leads on to the question of roads and highways, and car parks: the location of new highways outside densely built-up areas, the possibilities offered by slum clearance or reclamation.

At this point, the general aims of the conservation policy should be settled, as it has implications for the rest of the town. Should a particular area be conserved? How extensive should it be? To give it an appropriate setting, how should the immediately adjoining area be treated?

These wider implications may prove contentious: finding other sites for proposed large new buildings, for car parks, and for highway developments; relocating markets; building tunnels if the area is too large to be by-passed. These 'spillover' costs may be very high and must be assessed early if the conservation decision is to be realistic.

1. Co-ordination
No public works, redevelopment of buildings and so on should be undertaken locally until the detailed plan has been worked out. This implies that the plan must be made rapidly and not impose unreasonable delays on activities responsible for other works the community may urgently need.

2. Inventory
Streets, buildings, archaeological sites, gardens and cultural property generally should be listed and graded; the inventory should be transferred to maps, showing the full extent of the properties to be conserved, including trees and adjoining lands. It must show any spaces left for new development, and the degree to which traffic and parking can be allowed. The area may already have too much of both, and have to ban all but essential delivery traffic — perhaps even confining that to specific hours.

3. Extensions
The area may adjoin a development estate or itself be subject to considerable pressure; *e.g.* to provide tourist accommodation. Is co-existence possible?

The extensions must not distort. For example, extensions and uses which generate traffic on both sides of the conservation area would inevitably lead to a demand for facilities to allow cross traffic. On the other hand, new roads could be planned in such a way as to stimulate economic and social vitality in the area, and actually promote conservation. It may be preferable to site new hotels — and particularly, large hotels — near rather than in the area. Larger shops and supermarkets are probably best outside also.

Height, design, and layout should harmonise with those in the conserved area.

4. New uses for old buildings
New uses may have to be found for old buildings. A conserved area should not be a dead area. Social and economic activity must be sustained and encouraged, selectively, and new buildings must be designed to fit in, in scale and style, with existing ones. Sites for them may be found by removing ugly or unsuitable structures or additions.

The main difficulty will be to select uses which do not involve vehicular traffic; and internal modernisation may be costly. Otherwise, old town centres can be highly attractive and many become much sought after as exclusive residential districts (*e.g.* St Germain-des-Prés in the Paris Latin Quarter).

An interesting Yugoslav experiment accompanied the restoration of Diocletian's Palace in Split. Enterprises wanting centrally located offices and such institutions as an adult education college paid for the restoration of a section of the palace that they could use as premises. Some purists object to this, but the result is imaginative, sensitive and socially intelligent, and funds were found which would otherwise not have been available.

Some buildings are more adaptable than others. Monasteries can become hotels. Almost any structure can be adapted for use as offices, and historic quarters are particularly popular with solicitors, architects, estate agents and other professional people.

If the area is to be lively and animated, a good deal of ground floor space should be used for restaurants, cafés and small shops. This is desirable for locals, and essential for tourists.

5. Major monuments
There should be a continuous programme (probably spreading over many years) for churches, palaces and public buildings. Some will be preserved simply as monuments. This needs no economic justification. Nevertheless, domestic and foreign tourists may bring in immediate revenue (admission charges) and indirectly benefit shopkeepers and hotels. On the other hand, tourists often travel in large coaches, and want to get as near as possible. It may not be easy to arrange parking and access as they would like.

6. Services and amenities
The work of establishing a preserved area should be tackled, sector by sector, as part of a carefully tailored comprehensive plan.

So, if subsidies are available to bring dwellings up to modern standards, there will be plenty of demand for any houses renovated. Better-off families, with children, may prefer to move out to green belt areas. Students are always in search of cheap accommodation. Business and professional people are usually glad to buy or rent offices and living accommodation in restored historic quarters, and may sometimes undertake restoration themselves.

Urban life has its own environmental and social attractions. These are enhanced if people both live and work in the same area; they acquire a sense of civic responsibility which is likely to be the best long-term guarantee that the quality of living there will be preserved. This is particularly important in the case of historic towns.

Plans for conservation and development vary with the character of the places concerned; the latter can be divided into four main groups.

1. small historic towns and villages
2. historic quarters in large towns and cities
3. towns and cities which are themselves historic
4. historic groups, sites, palaces and so on.

Four examples will illustrate each of these categories:

1. Small Historic Towns and Villages

Historic towns and villages can be considered for conservation either individually or in groups. As populations grow and have to be accommodated, their particular character may be threatened; if situated in coastal or particularly attractive areas, there is likely to be an influx of tourists. As a farming population continues to leave the land and find work elsewhere, villages in many parts of Europe are subtly changing character. Even where they remain, farmers may sell their old, badly-equipped but picturesque houses and cottages, being more concerned with their defects than their charms. They prefer to build modern villas. Their old homes are eagerly bought up by weekenders from the cities.

In historic towns and villages, as the normal cycle of replacement and renewal takes place, there is a considerable danger that the character will change unless the changes or extensions are carefully planned.

Example – Hvar Island, Yugoslavia

A study of this island with a view to tourist development was undertaken as part of the United Nations South Adriatic Project. The island consists mainly of a mountain ridge rising out of the sea, with a heavily indented rocky coast, and many small shingle beaches. There are four small coastal towns of great beauty, and a number of villages. The villagers grow vines and lavender. The island has catered for tourists for over a century, but there are hotels only in the four towns. The greater part of the island creates an impression of remoteness and tranquillity.

Three possibilities were considered:

First, an airport could be built on the only piece of flat land on the island. Local opinion was favourable, as the airport would allow the island to compete for tourists. Even the most rapacious agreed, however, that most tourists might be discouraged by a jet aircraft landing or taking off every fifteen minutes and clearing the church tower in one of the historic towns by a bare five metres.

The second possibility, also favoured by local opinion, was to provide facilities which would encourage tourists to come with their cars. On investigation, this was also ruled out. Building roads in very difficult territory would have required heavy investment. The roads themselves would have ruined the natural landscape, and the hilly nature of the island made it unsuitable for people who might want to camp.

It was decided to adopt the third possibility and concentrate on attracting selected tourists who could come by hydrofoil from Split Airport, which is right beside the sea. This would be a convenient and even exciting trip, taking only forty-five minutes. The number of cars reaching the island would never be more than it could take without changing its character. Hvar would still be seemingly remote but in fact convenient, a combination much in demand but increasingly difficult to find; this happily combines economic interest with environmental preservation.

An estimate was then made of the island's resources: the coast line, possible sites for tourist accommodation, water supply, and the capacity of the towns and villages to expand without destroying their traditional relationship to the sea and the landscape. Capacity to expand on these conditions was not very large.

It was then decided to relate all development to a central spine road with short spurs, creating small tourist resorts close to the four existing towns, and leaving a large part of both the coast and the interior free as before.

From this point on, it was possible in planning to get down to items which can be specified, measured and numbered: tourist beds required, sites for new buildings, other services, standards as regards floor space and space around buildings, accommodation for cars, demand for water, electricity and so on.

Once the basic decisions had been taken, the quality of the final result depended largely on the skill and ability of the designers and planners.

2. Historic Quarters in Large Towns and Cities

Most European cities are already historic. They have industries and services. They also have historic buildings and parks and other open spaces, all of which may be threatened as the demand increases for sites, redevelopment, and roads that can take constantly increasing traffic.

Historic quarters in such cities are important to inhabitants and visitors alike. The dramatic contrast of old and new gives the cities part of their distinctive character. Yet survival is constantly threatened by the pressures that prosperity creates.

Example – Central Liverpool

The centre of Liverpool, serving a metropolitan area containing one and a half million people, was mostly built during the nineteenth century for nineteenth-century needs. Although it contains buildings and groups of the highest architectural importance, from the nineteenth century and earlier, it was somewhat run down and unsuitable for present-day pedestrian and car traffic.

The best buildings are mostly in the centre, which also contains the headquarters of the banking, shipping, insurance and other services of a major mercantile centre and international port. The enterprises in question wanted in many cases to pull down the existing buildings and redevelop their valuable central sites, using a much higher office density.

Some of the best buildings would have disappeared: Cockerell's Bank of England and the Norwich Union Insurance building, both distinguished examples of neo-classical architecture; redevelopment in the adjoining Castle Street would have destroyed the scale of the street itself and reduced the eighteenth-century domed Town Hall to insignificance.

It was essential to retain these important buildings. It was still possible for the owners to modernise and improve the interiors without affecting the external architecture. Extra office accommodation could be provided close-by by redevelopment on equally convenient sites which did not have the same architectural value.

Limitations were accordingly imposed which meant that redevelopment would not significantly increase the amount of accommodation on the same site, while much more generous height limits were allowed in the new office redevelopment area.

This policy was at first sharply challenged by the property owners and developers, but has succeeded. Many of the Castle Street buildings have been cleaned and renovated, and all of them have been retained. Two blocks away, very large office buildings are under construction. Conservation and development have been reconciled.

3. Towns and Cities which are Themselves Historic

Towns like Venice, Dubrovnik, Bath or Isfahan present a special problem in themselves. The past dominates the present. Tourists are essential to prosperity and not just a marginal source of income. The first consideration of the municipal authorities is to conserve their monuments, streets and squares. As building costs rise, it becomes more expensive to adapt or modernise existing buildings. Traffic has to be limited or diverted (*e.g.* the proposal in Bath to have traffic pass through a tunnel under the town).

Some of the cities mentioned are self-contained masterpieces. The cost of maintaining them is correspondingly high but, if intelligently used, the tourist trade can be enlisted in the cause of conservation.

Example – Isfahan. (See also Chapter 8 dealing in detail with the history and problems of the city).

By its unity, and the quality of its monuments, mosques, *caravanserai* and bridges, Isfahan is as important as Venice. It is a bustling and growing city of half a million people, capital of an important region. On the outside, seen from a street or a desert, Islamic architecture often appears deceptively plain and simple, but the surface decoration of the architecture itself may be astoundingly rich, and the disciplined geometry often masks interiors in which the most important spaces are open to the sky. Mosques, minarets and domes may be found along irregular narrow streets. Plain walls of houses have their own charm in the same streets, which are used mainly by people on foot and pack-donkeys.

In the old quarters, streets are mostly unpaved, compacted earth. In older times their narrowness discouraged incursions by large bodies of armed men. Today they are equally effective in discouraging the motor car. Such quarters may lie just behind busy new boulevards. A continuous succession of closed courtyards, single-storey lines, and buildings at a uniform height can produce an extraordinary impression of quietness and privacy. They provide an enviable setting for shrines and monuments and, even if improvements are necessary, an equally satisfactory living quarter.

Planned expansion.
During the next twenty-five years, Isfahan and similar cities must, while conserving their character, modernise and expand. New large jet aircraft and the reduced cost of packaged holidays are greatly increasing the number of tourists now travelling. Iran is well placed on the world's air routes to benefit. As in other countries it has resorts and facilities for skiing, hunting and other recreations. Its cultural heritage is the unique feature it can offer tourists. Tourists going to Iran are likely to be interested in both history and architecture, and a visit is hardly conceivable without seeing Isfahan.

Extra facilities and a certain degree of modernisation are necessary to cope with the requirements of tourists, and the increased prosperity and growth in the town itself and the neighbourhood. This growth has a number of causes.

a) The continuous development of Isfahan itself as the main regional centre for services, administration, education (including a new technical university), entertainment, recreation and culture.

A souk in Isfahan

b) Better rail communications and a new airport.

c) The development of hydro-electric resources, and irrigation projects.

d) The industrial development which has followed the establishment of a new steel works at Riz.

Where development can take place.

At present, there is little traffic congestion, and the roads and bridges serving central Isfahan are adequate. Extensive redevelopment in the centre would destroy this balance. But even outside the centre, development must be carefully controlled. Four bridges link Isfahan to its southern suburbs; three are historic monuments and cannot be widened without altering them completely. Additional new bridges within the town would damage, if not destroy, the superb, open meadow park setting of the city and the view of the existing bridges. They would also be very expensive to build. Accordingly, no major new developments should be allowed south of the river, so as to prevent increasing the load on the existing bridges.

But the difficulty of loading too much traffic on to the boulevards and the bridges they serve also applies if major development is allowed northwards. If development is allowed to the north it should be confined in one direction only, either to the east or to the west. Otherwise a whole network of east-west roads would have to be provided. It is clear that people cannot be compelled to live and work in the same part of a city. Mobility is a condition of social and economic development.

To confine the expansion of a city to development in one direction only needs strong measures, positive as well as negative. The more rapidly a large new residential and industrial district develops, the sooner can it provide its own centre. The existence of this new centre would lessen the need or desire for travel to the old centre of Isfahan and so lessen traffic pressures.

Brief surveys of this kind define the safeguards that are essential to prevent the destruction of the character of historic towns by thoughtless modernisation schemes.

4. Historic Groups, Sites, Palaces, and so on

Monuments such as Persepolis, Teotihuacan, Stonehenge, the Alhambra, Versailles, Pompeii, Ankor Wat are amongst the highest achievements of the cultures which produced them. They need special attention — sometimes even international aid. Each may combine several features: museum, archaeological site, location of *son et lumière* or other festivals. Administration, maintenance

An eleventh century church at Talmot (Vendée), France

and policing may be very costly.

Most of the problems of conserving such monuments and their particular environment arise from the fact that they are precious objects in themselves and attract vast numbers of visitors.

Example – Pyramids of Giza

At the request of Unesco and the Egyptian authorities, a survey was made of the setting and surrounding of the Pyramids of Giza, with a view to delineating a zone where new construction should be prohibited and proposing regulations to govern urbanisation in the surrounding area.

Even the pyramids might lose something of their majesty against a background of factory chimneys, suburban development, car parks or activities of a nearby airport.

On the other hand, it is unrealistic to imagine that the area around the pyramids will continue more or less empty forever. Societies change, populations expand and the pyramids, like all tourist attractions, attract ever-growing numbers of visitors. A visit to the Middle East without a visit to Egypt and its antiquities is almost inconceivable. And among the attractions the pyramids of Giza are both striking and accessible, being very close to Cairó. How can the facilities needed for this influx of tourists be provided?

The best solution seemed to be to lay down a set of principles which would remain valid, and accordingly applicable, as conditions continued to change. This seemed better than to propose a plan which would almost certainly prove to be too rigid within a comparatively short time. Together, the principles constitute a concept which summarises the general situation; the details are provided at any one time by taking account of the particular conditions which then apply.

The conclusions can be summarised as follows:

a) Three more or less conflicting requirements have to be satisfied:
1. Egyptologists, staff from the Antiquities Department, art historians and other specialists naturally prefer a quiet academic atmosphere.
2. Tourists seek free access, and many ancillary facilities.
3. Greater Cairo needs space for urban expansion.

b) The local environment is created by three factors:
1. The pyramids, tombs, temples and monuments themselves.
2. The combined effect they create on this particular flat site.
3. The relationship of this site to the desert on one side and a green valley on the other.

c) Means have to be found which will both satisfy the requirements and enhance the Pyramids of Giza as a monument.

d) This can best be done by treating the pyramids as a room within a setting. Visitors to the pyramids and the monuments are like visitors entering a quiet room; facilities they may need are concentrated near but outside the room.

e) The desert and the valley provide the setting. Skilful use must be made of topography to ensure that the growth of tourist facilities does not spoil this setting.

f) The concept should be broken down into constituent parts, each of which will become the subject of a planning study.

g) The setting as a whole should be declared a conservation area and an authority set up with the necessary resources and technical staff to implement these proposals.

2. ANXIETIES OF CITY DWELLERS

Hans Foramitti and Maximilian Piperek

For residents of cities, the problems of their lodgings, with the immediate environment, are far more important psychologically than the difficulties of streets and traffic. The principle of durability of domicile merits foremost consideration — as it received in practice in cities of Europe in their early times.

It was then the custom to maintain in cities the form and the quality of buildings, and without frequent internal change. And the great courtyards that gave access to buildings kept their structure. (Outside, however, there was certain to be change, for reasons we can recognise today: traffic problems are older than even Roman roads. Leonardo da Vinci studied roads. The Emperor Charles VI had roads widened for the needs of fast steeds and coaches passing one another. Sometimes towns were called upon to widen main arteries and enlarge squares despite their ramparts.)

Fairly constant standards governed the internal arrangement of courtyards, the access to various parts of the buildings, the width of pathways for pedestrians, inner drives for horsemen and vehicles, clearance for carriages, spaces for hawkers, the height and width of passages and doorways. The dimensions of rooms, stairways, passages — usually related to the height of a man. As climate, environment and conditions of life varied from place to place, so also did architectural forms, styles of art, and regional and ethnological customs; but the scale and proportions of buildings remained fairly constant.

In many countries, several generations of the same family lived and worked together, and this continued until the industrial revolution, when the demands of labour uprooted people and herded them together as a new proletariat in cities. Nowadays, people are increasingly leaving the land, where machines have replaced manual labour; and more and more people find employment in the tertiary sector in towns and cities.

Any change in occupation demands an effort of adaptation. Despite all that has been learned on the subject, and all the studies that have been made, economic necessity still forces people to move to less healthy surroundings, a hostile environment, and worse working conditions. Older, or even ancient buildings, sometimes survive as islands or small villages, but the concrete jungle steadily advances: to the speculator, the profit he can make from the site is more important than the survival of the buildings on it. There is plenty of evidence to show that the desire to see these old buildings survive has more solid justification than sentimental nostalgia. However, the evidence is less easy to display tangibly than a speculator's profit in a balance sheet.

Between 1950 and 1970, some two thousand case studies were made in Vienna with a view to investigating the sociological and psychological problems that result from unsatisfactory housing and living conditions; in each case, an average of two and a half hours were spent in consultations, tests and examinations.

Psychological Needs

From the earliest times, man has placed screens around his fragile and threatened existence, including clothing and dwellings to protect him from the environment and the weather. These screens have also been psychological or imaginary — a physical screen having a magical, emotional or religious counterpart. The various parts of a dwelling are themselves charged with meaning; and interposed between the self and the outside world was the family, the clan or the tribe. Various signs helped to allay anxieties caused by a threatening world: the limits marked by a furrow, the Druidic star or the sun, wheels on the beams of half-timbered houses, the lintels of main doors.

In this respect, the dwelling house, as the setting for the family, is of capital psychological importance. Its every detail acquires significance as the life of the individual proceeds. The importance of first impressions in the build-up of the psyche is well known. In one case out of three, a person's earliest memories will relate to features of his home and its immediate surroundings.

We shape our abode, and it shapes us. Changes in the environment, in an urban site, in the functions of a building, may set in motion a mechanism of inter-relationships which demands an effort of adaptation that may often exceed the psychic capabilities of certain of the people subjected to it. An undue obligation to adapt causes stress, and stress is common in great blocks of modern flats which nevertheless, are often put up in an attempt to provide, at a reasonable rent, facilities which people want — natural light, ventilation, central heating, lifts, sanitation, practical kitchens.

The figures afforded by the Vienna case studies of 1950-70 are alarming. One subject in four had serious psychological problems attributable to their living conditions (8 per cent were regarded as psychopaths).

Table 1

Symptoms	Percentages	Percentage increase after 10 years
Lack of concentration	18	3
Agitation and feverishness	18	4
Loss of memory	14.5	0.5
Loss of contact with nature	11	3.5
Neurosis	11	1
Psychopathic tension	11	2

With the exception of loss of memory, all these symptoms are increasing rapidly, and in some cases alarmingly. Other symptoms were found in 5 to 10 per cent of cases:—

Table 2

Symptoms	Percentage	Percentage change after 10 years
Thought and judgment reduced to simple stereotypes	9	+1
Lack of self-confidence	9	+1
Tendency to over-excitement	7.5	−0.5
Fear, anxiety	7.5	+0.5
Marked loss of psychic energy	6	(no change)
Failure to establish contact	6	−0.5
Tendency to scattered thought and inattention	5	(no change)

Although the percentage change is slight with regard to over-excitement, fear and anxiety, these affect over 7 per cent of cases, and lead to further complications, as a result of conflicts with other persons in the community in which the affected persons live and work. Again, the reduction of thought and judgment to simple stereotyped reactions means an appalling impoverishment of the individual, a lack of sensibility; and it may even lead to criminal acts.

In a third group (Table 3), particular attention should be paid to the tendency to aggression; a strong upward trend will shortly transfer the people concerned to those included in Table 2.

Table 3

Symptoms	Percentage	Percentage change after 10 years
Aggressive tendencies	4	+2
Over-intellectualisation	3	−0.5
Indifference towards values	3	no change
Depressive states	3	−0.5
Negative attitudes	2.5	no change

These findings must now be examined in greater detail. The need to feel protected has been common to mankind in all ages, and applies in a special way to the place chosen or accepted as a dwelling. A cavern, a roof, a tent, a place where the back was not exposed to attack by an enemy, allowed a human being to sleep, to rest, to prepare his food, to make tools. In 90 per cent of individuals, this primitive need survives and dominates many others. A person who is well balanced no longer fears attacks by foes, or the weather, but may be susceptible to the strains and intrusions of modern life — noise, traffic, over-work. Disregarding new dangers (such as pollution), health and physical existence are no doubt less vulnerable than in the past. But in other ways, man is sometimes more to be pitied than his distant forebears.

Pollution by noise and sound

Subjection over a long period to vibrations and sound can be extremely damaging; even without measuring instruments, a specialist can identify the noise coefficient which represents a danger to normal hearing. If two people talking in normal tones across a table in a restaurant or office can no longer understand one another, protective equipment becomes necessary. Even if the ears are shielded, a helmet may be needed to protect the bones of the cranium if the noise is particularly loud. Walls, floors, ceilings and doors can be soundproofed; windows can be double-glazed; typewriters can be placed on mats which absorb vibration; but the majority of such measures are costly and to be really effective, should be planned at the building stage. Rigid construction, in reinforced concrete or steel, creates bridges of heat, noise and vibration. Thin walls and partitions may well provide the minimum insulation stipulated by building regulations, but usually prove inadequate, to cope with the volume of sound that is actually generated. Heating can be reinforced; insulation against heat losses can be improved by thickening partitions; but noise is much more difficult to control.

The fear of being overheard by indiscreet ears can cause nervousness. Adequate protection against this is usually provided by the thick walls and floors of older buildings, and courtyards with shrubbery which absorbs sound. Modern buildings are usually less fortunate.

Daylight

Building regulations may impose minimum standards of natural light, and modern architects may use large panes and glass walls to provide it in abundance. As against this there is the anxiety of people who fear prying eyes and the invasion of their private lives. A vast living room may be convenient for receiving guests, but other rooms must be sacrificed to provide it; in fact, various rooms may be eliminated to provide a single area which serves for eating, rest, reading, entertainment and work. It is arguable that these multi-purpose rooms are a fundamentally mistaken concept. On the other hand, it may be added that apartments in countries like Austria designed to accommodate three generations of a family simultaneously and some domestic help, now seem over-sized for modern requirements.

Vibration

Vibration contributes to neuroses. Vibrations can become intolerable if they continue indefinitely or if, by ill-chance, the frequency of some domestic object corresponds to the frequency of an external vibration, causing resonance. A dripping water tap can be maddening. The electric motor which operates a lift, or vibrations from outside caused by cars, trains, tramways, and so on, are felt more readily in concrete and steel structures than in buildings with walls of heavy masonry. The same degree of absorption could be obtained in the newer buildings, but the cost is usually considered excessive.

Odours

Odours can be not merely disagreeable but positively harmful. Heavy industry is often a notable offender, although smaller works may be even more difficult to control. People may hesitate to open windows on hot summer nights, or become used to smells which nevertheless continue to have their undesirable effects on physical and mental health. The influence of odours is included here among the list of causes of psychopathic conditions.

The lurking threats

The dangers which threaten existence have in some cases changed in outward form, but man may need a secluded refuge as desperately today as did his primitive ancestors. He is assaulted by a multitude of sensations he would like to exclude from that corner of the universe he wants to reserve for his own use. His zone of contemplation should not be too brightly lit, should include a quiet corner, be sheltered from view and sound, and be closed in by walls of strong appearance and a solid floor. A failure to establish defences may result in aggressiveness, bad temper, hypersensitivity, morosity. The preference for a corner or niche, close to a substantial partition, is not so far fetched, even today. Earthquakes, explosions and fires occur as frequently as they ever did; and in these catastrophes, when floors collapse, corner fragments close to walls usually survive.

Fire
The larger the openings, in the shape of doors and windows either within a house or giving on to the outside, the greater are the difficulties of fire control. Whatever the other considerations involved, smaller openings represent a greater safeguard against fire and satisfy certain psychological needs; fire risks are further decreased by protuberances above and below the opening. Certain building regulations stipulate horizontal projections of a minimum width of 60 centimetres on multi-storied buildings that have flat outer surfaces. In older buildings, the relation between openings and solid wall surfaces usually represented a satisfactory compromise between fire precautions and the need for ventilation and light. Pediments and buttresses prevent flames from penetrating readily through windows, and provide obstacles from floor to floor; if the fire starts within the building, the intake of air is lessened. Metal blinds, and even wooden shutters which will burn, also help to lessen the intake of air.

In the older parts of cities, buildings tend to be huddled together and it can be difficult to open up clear avenues as a precaution against the spread of fire. On the other hand, former ramparts or water-courses may have been replaced by wide tree-lined boulevards or green spaces. In addition to their visual advantages, these are important elements in fire control.

For security reasons, it is always desirable that walls be thicker than the minimum necessary for purely structural reasons. Thick walls, rooms of moderate proportions, each as far as possible serving a single purpose only, natural daylight coming through windows of reasonable size, and heavy solid floors not only provide a comforting sense of safety but are in fact safer. Many old houses in Europe are built of brick or ashlar. Walls frequently have two facings, with an intervening space filled with rubble. Half-timbering is often seen, and houses may be built entirely of wood. Bricks resist fire admirably. Even they begin to disintegrate at high temperatures; thick walls of brick are affected to a proportionately lesser extent and their stability is not endangered. The mortar which holds the bricks together may be carried away under pressure from fire hoses, but many tests and studies indicate that the unaffected core of the wall continues to provide support.

Wood will retain its bearing capacity for as long as those sections which have not been destroyed by fire can stand up to the strains laid on them. Generous dimensions accordingly lengthen the interval available for successful fire fighting.

The same, unfortunately, cannot be said of modern materials. Reinforced concrete buildings are endangered at temperatures of $300° - 400°C$, and collapse at $600° - 700°C$. Unless technical safeguards which are costly and seldom used are provided, steel reaches a danger point at $200°C$; at $500°C$ it loses half its power of resistance, and at $600° - 700°C$, practically all resistance. The risk is greatest in the case of skyscrapers, or additional storeys superimposed on an old building. While the materials may be fireproof, furnishings and other objects could feed a fire for hours and create the temperature levels just mentioned. Many synthetic substances are readily combustible and, once set alight, are difficult to extinguish. The insulation afforded by plastic on electrical leads drops sharply at temperatures above $500°C$. In a fire, vapours and acids attack these leads and cause short-circuits which in turn start secondary fires.

Buildings are also set on fire deliberately by criminal acts or attacks in war. Towards the end of World War II, 60 per cent of the bombs dropped on towns were incendiary. In major city fires, the rate of damage is in direct proportion to the density of construction. When buildings occupy 20–30 per cent of the surface area, destruction may amount to 65 per cent; when the density is 40 per cent, the rate of destruction may be at least 80 per cent.

Theft and housebreaking

Burglars may not hesitate to endanger the lives of those who stand in their way. Aggression of this nature is a constant fear, especially to people who live alone or are momentarily without company – in an isolated cottage, for example. Here again, thick walls, solid floors and ceilings, heavy doors, metal grilles and so on, are good for morale and help to discourage intruders. Fear is often, and perhaps usually, exaggerated, but is nonetheless real for that, and creates a craving for reassurance.

The vast majority of people want a home which is tranquil and reassuring. This need is accentuated in people who are hypersensitive, who are overwhelmed by the pace of modern living, or who simply want to feel safe by their own hearth and have friends without being compelled to live in constant contact with too many other people. Houses in old quarters often satisfy many of these conditions, and can often be fully modernised for much less than it would cost to put up an equivalent in a modern building.

Social relations

Most of the people interviewed in the case studies wanted security and protection from various kinds of irritations, but were frightened of living in isolation. It was not so much that they wanted contacts, as the assurance that they could easily make such contacts if and when they so desired. Here, the telephone has an obvious role to play.

In older towns, the architecture often provided an extraordinary background for the life that was carried on in the shops, streets and market squares. There is a growing trend nowadays to reserve such places exclusively for pedestrians. Shopkeepers were at first reticent, but in many cases found that the more familiar and genial atmosphere created turned casual purchasers into regular customers.

Light and a view

Some people are happy only in restful surroundings: a park, a garden, by the view of a landscape or lake. Others prefer the animated life of a busy street. There is no perfect compromise. But while most people like to have some view from their windows, it is important to avoid falling into the error committed by many builders who believe they can deal with a complex problem by providing large expanses of glass.

Buildings in narrow streets should not be allowed to exceed a certain height. There is a case for removing the upper storeys subsequently added to buildings in such streets. Here the desiderata of the safety expert match those of the psychiatrist. Low buildings, with courtyards, if possible with some shrubs, plants and flowers, constitute many safeguards against conflagrations. Buildings which have openings front and back, or at both ends, allow through ventilation and, in case of emergency, allow rescue services impeded at one side to enter from the other. Here again there is a link between physical safety and health and psychological safety and health.

Nature

Many of the people surveyed valued a contact with nature above the comforts and other advantages that modern civilisation can provide. Deep window embrasures designed to be filled with flowers were characteristic of the Biedermayer period in Vienna; and many neo-classical frontages carried miniature replicas of the vast conservatories and winter gardens that were still in fashion in the early twentieth century. Families kept dogs, cats and birds. But the green spaces, trees and flowerbeds that survive are a a poor substitute for the more generous nature for which so many people long.

Moving waters and unencumbered shores become more and more
difficult to find near cities. Those which have not been obliterated by
built-up areas are tamed because it is no longer possible to
tolerate the floods and high tides which formerly did little damage
in open country.

The survey seems to indicate that this distancing of nature harms
the personality in many ways: gradual diminution of initiative and
creative thought; loss of sensitivity to primary values; false intellectualism,
psychosis and psychic tensions; emotional disturbances; negative
attitudes.

It is ironic to think that, in a modern city, so much damage can be
caused, partly at least, because it is impossible to take a quiet walk,
lie down in grass, dig a patch of soil, pick a flower.

Dirt

The extent to which some cities use their rivers and streams as
sewers and drains is horrifying. Industries pollute vast areas, and the
amounts of rubbish and household refuse grow overwhelming. This
general poisoning of the environment is not only a danger to health
but a psychological menace. A civilised town should foster a local
patriotism and strengthen the bonds between a man and his town and
his fellow citizens; instead, the modern town stifles in its own dirt
and breeds only a desire to escape. Those who, seeking air and
cleanliness, desert the centre for the suburbs, just accept many
drawbacks, including the long daily trek to and from their place of work.
Municipalities which fail to tackle their pollution and traffic problems
will soon reach saturation point if present trends continue, and will
inevitably lose many active and constructive citizens whose cooperation
is essential if the city is to be not only modern, but thought of as a
place worth living in.

Nomads

The modern wage-earner will readily migrate. A new category of
industrial nomads is being created, people prepared to move to
wherever wages are highest and prospects best. The survey indicates that
few such people are capable of standing the strain of constant
adaptation without danger to themselves and their families. After all,
there is a family relationship between 'habitation' and 'habit'. Some
symbol of continuity is especially necessary for the industrial nomad,
and even for the seasonal worker who returns home after doing a
spell abroad.

The longing for stability

The following Table shows symptoms found among people interviewed who had failed to satisfy this longing for stability.

Table 4

Symptoms	Percentage
Depression	46
Anxiety	41
Loss of mental powers	33
Loss of skills	33
Loss of memory	27
Over-emotionalism	24
Loss of self-confidence	19
Thoughts of suicide	8

Of the total interviewed, 25 per cent were classified as sensitive or introvert; when they succeeded in doing so, these took six to eight months to adapt. Others took two to three months. While young people and extroverts most readily adapt, they are far less open and impressionable, and have few cultural interests. On the other hand, it is the sedentary individuals who are most likely to give a city its civic and cultural character. Their contribution is vital to artistic and cultural life, which may be based on the city but extend over a whole province or country. It is hardly a coincidence that such people are particularly at home in old quarters which have been renovated and brought back to life.

Architecture and materials have their own symbolic significance. Hewn stone, for example, is an embodiment of stability. Certain shapes convey a notion of solidity, *e.g.* blocks of masonry, massive pillars, heavy stone supports for balconies, and so on. The same applies to furniture: an old family chest or a portrait help to link past and present.

All things have their season
The juxtaposition of past and present takes place quite naturally in family dwellings inhabited by successive generations. Furniture from different periods reflects the tastes (or resources) of its purchasers. When a style is abandoned for a newer style, the first may be regarded initially as out of date but later as historic, at which point vestiges from earlier styles may become outstandingly valuable — the objects of poorer quality having been gradually eliminated. Things loved by grandparents may be loathed by their children but be cherished again by their grandchildren.

A home to live in
One temporary solution for dealing with a chronic housing shortage

is to provide the greatest possible number of medium-priced apartments capable of accommodating at most two adults and one child. If the couple continue to have children, this obviously can not be a permanent home. The industrial nomads mentioned above constitute another factor that tends to make the apartment a temporary home at best. On the other hand, older people tend to sub-let their larger flats in order to cover the cost of upkeep. There is thus a growing population of sub-tenants living in other people's furnishings. The old ideal of a residence as a place in which one is born, lives and dies in old age may be almost obsolete, but there should be at least some possibility for people who so desire to be able to settle down and to create a home with some reasonable hope of being able to remain there.

A roof of one's own

A natural reflex, within the home, is to deny access to strangers. In a household of three adults, if one is the mother-in-law, conflict is traditional, especially if the living space is restricted.

Ideally, every child, or at least children of the same sex, should have a separate room; in these, they should be free to arrange the furnishing as they wish. People who can afford it often buy or rent two apartments of different sizes, preferably on the same staircase and landing, one for the grandparents and the other for the young couple and their children. After the death of the grandparents, the two dwellings are merged, or else the smaller one is assigned to one of the children who marries. The young couple are frequently given some old pieces of furniture to which they have become particularly attached.

Where the desire for independence remains unfulfilled, it was found in the case studies that aggression developed, and tended to increase with age. In cramped quarters, forced co-habitation means that, from every point of view, self-expression is inhibited. Bad temper, a decline of interest in work and in life generally are matched by a growth of anxiety and fear.

Leisure

Children need to be able to move about; what they actually do is probably of secondary importance. For adults, work is often so mechanical and anonymous that they need some compensating activity in the home. It may incidentally be mentioned that organised leisure can be almost as monotonous as organised work. Gardening and hobbies provide important outlets. But how is it possible, in the average apartment block, to make noise or dust without disturbing others, to sing or play an instrument? Working hours are tending to grow shorter in industrial and commercial occupations. The extra free time may be used for purely leisure occupations; but it is also used to obtain a secondary source of income, by freelance work such as typing, translating, handicrafts, sewing which may be half-work, half-hobby.

Scale and proportion

It is important to avoid giving people the impression that they are living in barracks, with all the anonymity that that implies. As a general rule, therefore, blocks should not be too large, and be in reasonable proportion to each other and to their surroundings. It is no remedy to attempt to give character to an enormous structure by adding on ceramics, frescoes or pieces of sculpture afterwards. It is hard to decide whether some small houses that occasionally survive (perhaps temporarily) beside vast new blocks are funny or tragic. Vertical height certainly creates more psychological problems than horizontal extent.

Dimensions and proportions are just as important inside as out. Tall narrow rooms, and wide rooms with low ceilings, are equally to be avoided. Architects are well aware of the oppressive effect of architectural features which seem to close in on the inhabitant. The necessity of planning structures in relation to human height was well understood by Renaissance builders. Japan offers another interesting example: the traditional Japanese room was related to the height of a person sitting on the floor. Le Corbusier's modulator is a modern expression of the same principle. The use of natural materials, and the breakdown of masses and surfaces, bring architecture more into line with real human needs.

In architecture as in industry, mass production tends to produce sameness and monotony. But man needs recognisable landmarks. A deliberate mixing of roughly similar forms is sometimes regarded as a solution, but the survey indicates that the result is not so much variety as confusion. The individual feels that he does not belong, he loses touch and fails to establish neighbourly relations with those living around him. Where there are several blocks, the psychologist would suggest that each should have attractive and recognisable features (an arrangement of trees for example). Paths leading to shops, schools and so on from each block should also be identifiable rather than interchangeable, perhaps providing an optional route to the road or public transport line. They should, however, meet or cross from time to time to increase the choice and provide opportunities for meetings. And dead-ends are the negation of freedom of movement.

In this respect, the layout of many historic cities or quarters offers an enlightening contrast to that of modern blocks of buildings. The older city was usually centred, visibly and coherently, around a castle, a bridge, a square or the intersection of important highways. Main

54

streets led to smaller squares, each with its own function and character, with churches, fountains and other items that contributed to the individual character and movement. Formerly, lanes led off from the streets and were used by people and farm vehicles coming and going between the town and the fields, farms or workshops. The large and small squares of the town were focal points, meeting places and markets.

Much modern architecture prides itself on being functional. If it is functional, it is so in a very narrow sense. Form is a vital aspect of architecture, and form is outraged by a building which is put up without any consideration for its surroundings. Many buildings are falsely experimental, seeking to stand out from the surroundings at any cost instead of merging into them. New buildings and towns which are fortunate enough to have an old centre or historic quarter should above all be of sufficient architectural merit to stand up to comparison with the company they are to keep.

Irreplaceable loss

The survey points out that some irreplaceable sites have been destroyed for all time through grave errors of style, dimension or proportion. A town squanders inherited beauty at its risk and peril. A great deal of skilled artisans' work went into older buildings. Things were never completely identical, and variations of shape derived from variations of structure and the properties of natural materials (stone, wood, leather, ivory). Things so made had a value in themselves, apart from their completely utilitarian use, and these values man instinctively seeks in order to create and sustain the rhythm of his own life. It is highly dangerous, for both individuals and communities, if this psychic drive disappears. Marcel Jousse has written of the extent to which miming and gesture are fundamental factors in psychological development. This is as pertinent to the making of an artifact, and to its creator's pleasure, as to the satisfaction and appreciation of the user. The survey emphasised the importance people attach to colour — gravely impaired in towns by dirt and pollution. Natural colours arouse the deepest response, confirming in this the conservationists' insistence on their importance.

A different place

The home should provide a change from the utilitarian atmosphere of the workshop, office or laboratory. Appropriate heating, cooling or ventilation deals with only part of the climate of a home. An excess of smooth and shiny surfaces (plastics, plastified surfaces, glass, polished metal) is to be avoided; the survey showed very clearly how much importance people attach to things and objects which do in fact help to differentiate the home from the place of work. Prefabricated elements to which additions are made as further needs arise are amongst the causes of monotony. Variety is added by works of art, personal or family mementoes, travel souvenirs, books, items of folklore and even objects in bad taste. The need for such things is confirmed by the growing demand for good copies of old furniture, reproductions of paintings and drawings, art photographs and so on.

The psychologist and the safety expert are at one with the conservationist in recommending historic quarters as good places to live in. It has been found in Vienna that it is easier to restore and modernise old buildings than was at one time thought, and the cost of doing so is about 20 per cent less than that of demolishing and putting up a new building to give equivalent accommodation. The revitalisation of old areas is the quickest and least costly way of providing an element which humanises our ever-growing built-up areas. The scale of values applied in restoration is one that aims at producing a human architecture. Without sacrificing the benefits of modern civilisation, it respects old laws of symmetry and proportion, the unique character of works of art, and makes its contribution towards the restoration of an environment in which men can be mentally as well as physically healthy.

3. BACK TO THE AGORA!

Piero Gazzola

Our experience during the last few decades has shown that passive conservation, based on a strict aesthetic conception of cultural property, may in the best of cases prolong its life, but cannot really guarantee protection. For natural reasons and because of pollution resulting from industrialisation, the menace to its existence is always more or less near. Moreover, the enormous increase in population and improved living standards demand so much new installation as almost to nullify any attempt at passive protection.

A new approach is needed, taking cultural property in all its aspects (social and economic included) as something productive in our civilisation. For the deterioration of our environment, the degradation of the habitat, the spiritual turmoil which is at the root of the chronic anxiety in which we live, stem from the exaggerated faith we have placed in economists with their vision of economic progress in the most material and petty sense − more production and more income − as the cure-all for man's ills. Faced with the failure of the industrial civilisation the economists wished for, and the menaces to survival we have only recently been told about, all responsible people feel obliged to reconsider what they think and do. We conservationists have had to recognise that our form of protection is not enough: that all the goods of the earth must be reviewed and re-evaluated, so that they can be put to the best use on behalf of man, who resumes his place at the centre of our concern.

Cultural heritage is thus no longer something to be considered in the abstract but in relation to what it can contribute to the good of mankind. This cannot be purely economic, but must also comprehensively take in the cultural, the social, and even the poetic.

The conservation of historical centres has often been considered as a nostalgic dream for romantics. This was to some extent true, when conservation was mainly concerned only with facades and town squares. The approach must be more realistic and practical if, through the rehabilitation of old towns, the urban environment is to be made more human and habitable. The operation must not be simply skin deep but be social and cultural as well.

By their very nature, historic centres keep the contacts with the past and with the art and history they embody; the inhabitants subconsciously identify with the social and cultural atmosphere that surrounds them. When a town loses this quality of being an *agora,* a market and meeting place, it becomes sterile, and its society becomes de-urbanised rather than (as is often supposed) over-urbanised. It is in this sense that a revitalised historic centre can make urbanisation human by facilitating contacts between people and classes. It can become a key factor in good administration, not only through its historical associations, but through the truly modern urban function it performs, one that has no counterpart in a suburb or in the sprawling outskirts of a city.

The artificiality of new quarters humiliatingly expresses our ignorance or lack of perception of what people truly need. Hostile forms intimidate and condition us, prevent a response to the needs of body, soul and social life. They reflect an uneasy superficiality, a chronic frustration, the loneliness of the individual swallowed up in the crowd, and are one of the root causes of urban dehumanisation. The environment we are creating is an impersonal machine, soulless and unfeeling. In replacing what home once meant to people by a precarious mechanical efficiency, we make a blunder for which we pay dearly.

Not so long ago, the city seemed immune from the natural law which decrees that all things human are transitory. Forms changed without preventing the give-and-take between past and present which has characterised town planning and architecture down the centuries; due respect was paid to the natural environment, the town's structure and its dominant colour. The town centre fitted perfectly together. Around a compact central hub, behind its ramparts, secondary zones began to stretch outwards. Natural vegetation and crops circled the town, providing a green belt between the more densely populated central part and its outlying ramifications. The countryside penetrated into the town and the two together gave the environment its character. But nowadays, scores of ill-assorted buildings spring up on all sides, destroying and replacing the greenery.

A monument should always have its proper setting in which it can be seen to advantage. The setting may be a criss-cross of streets, a gap in a cluster of trees, or the satellite buildings which grow up around it; but it will always be something complex and delicate rather than a mere accumulation of miscellaneous objects.

Past and present, to the city, are the dialectics of history which it is up to us to conciliate. For the purposes of present-day life we must fashion a new language which takes account of both the social imperatives of today and the heritage of the past. We must judge objectively what we can make of an old town, made up of narrow, winding streets and buildings that are often dark and humid. It is better to be utilitarian than romantic, but without ignoring the poetry that emanates from a living urban entity. Not everyone recognises this, but it is an idea that is steadily gaining ground.

On the social side, it may be taken for granted that the idea of revitalising is now accepted as being the only way in which monuments and sites can be given a role in the modern life of both the individual and the community; this means an assessment of our needs and of the capacity of the monument and site to respond to them without losing any of their historical, aesthetic, urban-enhancing, or cultural qualities.

Revitalisation can hardly be considered in terms of short-term material returns; a monument or a group may simply not be adaptable in this way. The purpose may be to give it back its specific cultural role, and its historical and aesthetic function; but sometimes, it is when it has no evident practical role that the flavour of history and poetry it imparts does most to enrich our environment. In other words, it is not enough to find the solution which is best architecturally and technically.

However up-to-date or sophisticated the techniques used, any human intervention inevitably changes a monument; its physical condition may be improved, but something of its message is lost. Hence any kind of restoration, no matter how slight, demands an appreciation of values and a sensibility live to all the implications and to their total, final effect.

There is, for example, the patina that time imparts. The weathering which is partly its cause may at the same time damage, but the patina is something valuable that must at all costs be retained.

The modern town devoted mainly to industry and commerce in a way resembles a collection of places, offices and urban corridors which no doubt has a certain territorial and economic homogeneity. But very often, vital needs of people as members of the community are ignored. In the old town, by contrast, people feel freer and better — providing, of course, that it is not intersected by major roads nor swamped by chaotic traffic.

The suburbs and outskirts of cities tend to be particularly uninspiring. Younger people have little opportunity to make contact with others, and a lack of experience fosters either a certain narrow-mindness or a spirit of revolt — or perhaps both simultaneously. For this, society pays a heavy price.

The centre may be more attractive; but a town has to be considered and administered in all its parts. It has a certain layout which, quite apart from any question of monuments, has to be respected. Social and economic diversity cannot be brought about simply by demolishing outbuildings and accretions. The structure of a town is extremely complex. Its equilibrium is delicate, the result of complex stratifications which have probably taken place over centuries. Without a great deal of thought it cannot be properly comprehended, and major changes should be sanctioned only if they can be approved in the light of this kind of understanding. This is all the more true of changes in the older quarters; the aim must always be to preserve their charm undiminished, and indeed, wherever possible, to enhance it.

Certain historic towns are losing population; at the same time old quarters exert an undoubted attraction as places to live in. The paradox is only apparent. Recent studies have shown that, if people leave, it is largely because planners and authorities have not taken needed measures; and very often the panic expressed is, in origin, political and polemical. Depopulation does in fact occur in many urban areas at particular moments, but it is due primarily to a failure to adapt and keep buildings in good repair, and also, in certain instances, to ageing in the families and the fact that people are living longer. Planning is inadequate. Not enough one-family residences are provided; hence a housing shortage. The shortage is sometimes accentuated when mansions that had been divided up into smaller units are restored to their former condition. On the other hand, the first dwellings to be vacated are those which are least attractive, and depopulation by clearing slums is an absolutely essential step to urban rehabilitation.

But depopulation is definitely undesirable in two cases. First, when people are drawn to the outskirts by the uncontrolled spread of business or other occupations there; and secondly, when renewal in the centre is purely speculative, and houses are turned into offices, or working-class and middle-class accommodation is demolished to make way for luxury apartments. In this latter case, people are not leaving their town, they are being driven out by speculators.

Apart from the cases just mentioned, it is seldom that people leave their houses because of inadequate public administration if the houses are at all habitable; more often than might be supposed it is people themselves who resist speculation.

In a free market economy the State may subsidise new building but refuse to help owners with the upkeep of old houses. The latter fall into disrepair and their inhabitants move out to new quarters in the outskirts. Higher living standards make people more demanding; they want roomier dwellings, with more light and air than is available in the centre. Until the crowding caused by housing shortages that followed two world wars comes to an end, this moving out of populations should be welcomed. It is the only way in which houses can be renovated without moving too many people — an extremely costly operation — and in which accretions can conveniently be knocked down and sites restored.

There is a widely held but mistaken view that old quarters are not a good place to live in for normal families with children. Here again the fault lies with the public authorities. Provided they are kept in good repair, houses in such areas, as explained above, provide ideal accommodation from a human point of view. This is true both for its older residents and for people who move in and find it relatively easy to become assimilated into local community life. The old town offers cultural advantages not only for students and children but for people of all ages, and the public authorities should ensure that facilities for formal education, for both children and adults, are adequate to exploit these advantages.

In view of its social repercussions, the illogical splitting up of accommodation is another matter that deserves mention. When housing is badly managed and inspection lax, houses or apartments are split up after children have left home to marry. The final result is little better than a slum: more people are accommodated in the same space, when the contrary would have been expected and desirable.

The Marais district in Paris offers an interesting example of renovation. Most of the inhabitants were craftsmen and small shopkeepers who moved in at the end of the eighteenth century into mansions vacated when their aristocratic or upper class owners moved to new town houses in the Faubourg St Germain. The great drawing rooms were divided up by partitions to provide workshops and living rooms. Contrary to what might have been expected, there have been no disastrous consequences; when the partitions were recently removed again, most of the original decoration, plaster and paint-work was found to be preserved almost intact.

Under the Malraux Act, the occupants were obliged to leave — very much against their will, in fact — while the renovations were being carried out. They were entitled to be the first call on the accommodation once the operation was complete. However, as a result of the demolition of various outbuildings and accretions, the renewed quarter could accommodate only 60,000 out of its original 90,000 inhabitants.

There are two problems in such cases: to decide which inhabitants can return; and to find workshops and living accommodation elsewhere for the remainder.

It would be a mistake to underestimate the discontent aroused among people who are attached to the neighbourhood to which they have traditionally belonged, who are not rich, and who fear they will not be able to make a living elsewhere. So far as possible they must be able to make their homes again in the same district. In this respect at least, the depopulation which voluntarily takes place in certain historic centres should be welcomed as an opportunity to be seized.

More comfortable, with more light and air, but still retaining all their charm, the renovated dwellings would be much in demand — provided that the operation has not been carried out by speculators interested only in forcing up rents and providing accommodation for the better-off population who replace the original inhabitants. If the promoters are conscientious, however, and seriously and honestly interested, they can do a great deal to rehabilitate historic towns. It is a dangerous illusion to imagine that everything can be undertaken and financed by the public authorities. Such towns will to a large extent be saved, cleaned up and restored only if old buildings can be dealt with under social, economic and financial conditions applying in the case of new buildings.

Mansions and aristocratic residences must be considered apart. It is not easy to find a suitable modern use for the sumptuous salons, ballrooms and apartments. With decorations often as fragile as they are rich, a museum is one obvious use, but a town does not need all that many museums. Bankers and industrialists sometimes take over historic buildings as head offices for banks, insurance companies and the like. A limited number of rich or professional people may be able to afford the cost and upkeep; this applies in particular to those who have fled from the pollution, traffic and overcrowding of the modern city but might be glad to get back to the town again, in the human and civilised atmosphere of a renovated historic quarter.

Planning must from the outset take account of potential interests of this kind and allow maximum scope for private enterprise. Amongst other things, this will foster interest in each town's architectural heritage and in the environment in general — an interest which is becoming increasingly sharpened. People who decide and can afford to take over renovated historical buildings do not often leave them again for very long periods, and experience shows that this stability usually produces an excellent standard of upkeep.

There is general agreement nowadays regarding the desirability of comprehensive planning; within this framework, the revitalisation of historic centres appears profitable from every point of view, including the economic. The safeguarding of historic centres should be seen as an integral part of regional and urban planning as a whole. National planning is less likely to be subject to petty local interests, and better results can be obtained by treating the safeguard of cultural property as a problem which has obvious links with zoning and the provision of parks and open spaces. It may be noted that the countries most advanced in social and urban planning have for decades been earmarking enormous sums in their annual budgets for the acquisition of great tracts of agricultural land and forests against the day when population will increase still more rapidly, and the provision of leisure and recreation facilities will become still more urgent.

Seeing these two problems (the safeguarding of historic centres and the creation of vast green areas) together might provide a framework within which many extremely difficult problems could find solutions. Historic centres could be the poles of attraction in a dynamic housing policy.

A revitalisation scheme depends for success on having essential services already available: drainage, water, gas, electricity, telephone, public lighting and so on. A satisfactory solution must also have been found for the traffic and parking problems.

There are also implications for the tertiary sector (including shops), and social services, schools, cultural centres, libraries and markets. In the general distribution of the national revenue, this may mean allocating a larger share for local communities and municipalities, whose resources do not at present allow them to keep pace with modern life and new attitudes to living.

These problems are not insoluble, but must be treated together on a long-term basis if man is to be the be-all and end-all, as he should be, in this new conception of the environment.

Within this framework the planner must recognise the special place of the historic town or village. It may provide a community centre, especially in towns in which expansion is the absolute priority. In most cases, despite its limited size and limited building space, the old quarter may still provide the most suitable cultural and commercial centre — and even administrative capital.

It is, in any case important to move with caution, avoiding drastic or over-simplified solutions, first thinking very seriously about the real value of the old quarter and its possibilities, in general and in detail, as a potential *agora* or meeting point; for we have hitherto either neglected, or have been much to rough-and-ready, in appreciating the importance of its function.

Surveys in England and the Netherlands indicate that there are almost never any vacant apartments available in rehabilitated old quarters. As soon as an apartment is vacated, prospective new tenants appear at once — fortunately this is particularly true when the reconversion is good and all amenities are provided such as special attention to pedestrians, playgrounds, schools, wooded areas, car parks, shopping areas, and so forth.

Old districts, even unrestored, have a special attraction for old people who are looking not so much for low rents as for an environment that is human — something that is unavailable in new quarters. In this they are expressing their generation's rejection of a civilisation that overvalues economic advantages at the expense of basic human values.

For some years, economists and businessmen have also taken an increasing interest in the restoration of old quarters, particularly when the buildings are in good condition and reasonably immune from pollution. But one recurrent and somewhat intractable problem arises whenever an application is made for permission to transform ground-floor house-fronts. The hearing of applications should take account of all we have learnt of late about the role of streets and shopping areas as a community meeting place for the urban centre as a whole. Some research and study may still need to be done to convince all concerned — with statistics in support — of the advantages of maintaining a certain uniformity of style and decoration along a street, and a certain harmony between the lower and upper fronts.

One notion which deserves short shrift concerns the size of shop windows. If a shop is otherwise well laid out and appointed, the size of the windows will matter little. Again, contrary to what many shopkeepers feared, it has been found in most countries that the diversion of all traffic from certain streets and squares led to an increase in their business rather than the reverse.

Studies are being carried out to ascertain to what extent the historic centre provides a meeting place not only for the modern town that has grown up, but for the whole area around. The malaise in the anonymous, sprawling dormitory towns is all too obvious. They lack the catalyst which fosters social life, and which historic centres ideally provide, irrespective of any purely economic return (though this, of course, is not be be underestimated). They offer a most useful and humane means of drawing people back into society from an isolation which is perhaps one of the main, if imponderable, reasons of alienation and revolt among the working classes and the young.

The gulf between social categories in this kind of urban zoning imposed by industrialisation has isolated the individual in the megalopolis. Historic centres, revitalised physically and in spirit, could be one way of atoning for the error of supposing that we could turn men into cogs and, with overweening arrogance, obliterate, along with the tokens of the past, all spiritual values, and proclaim the almightiness of industrial progress and physical welfare.

Hitherto, planning authorities have approached the problem mainly in terms of real estate and space, almost wholly ignoring the social and spiritual factors. Even space has been considered in material terms: the economic value of the site decided, without any reference to the ecological implications; and urban renewal preferred to urban rehabilitation, because — in monetary terms — it is less costly.

The opposite view is taken by those whose interest is in architecture and in buildings, and by those who want to preserve historical monuments and cultural environments, who are concerned above all with the health of the individual and of the community in the broadest sense. To them in consequence, the rehabilitation of a city is less costly than its renewal.

We must, alas, admit that we have so far been ill-equipped to tackle the problems, and inept in seeking solutions. If our everyday actions find a reflecting mirror in the things that surround us, the reflection of ourselves that our physical environment provides is a sorry one indeed. We sometimes prefer to look at space rather than inhabit it. Our visual and aesthetic appreciation of monuments and of our environment, like our appreciation of the historical interest of a particular item in it, is wholly inadequate. It takes in only a part, sealed off in a sort of abstract and sterile limbo, passing over something more intimate and personal. Buildings and monuments give a place its character, its uniqueness, make it stand out in our eyes, and in our mind's eye, providing a nexus between what we are and the place of our existence which, to some extent, also moulds us.

'Dead' works are thus in reality the living embodiment of the individuality, the uniqueness of a historical site, and confirm the relationship between our transitory selves and the spirit of the place.

From this visual standpoint, conservation is rescue, a recovery of all that is most innately human of a lost equilibrium and wholeness.

New legislation will of course be necessary but also, and above all, a new and profound awareness of what we can properly expect of the places in which we live out our lives.

Between men and the cities they live in we must rediscover and remake a relationship that has deteriorated over the past sixty years. The city, *urbs* and *civitas,* must again become the *agora,* the gathering place, hub and heart of the community, an assembly and a place that offers never-ending opportunities for give-and-take between a person and his physical and social environment. Rediscovering those areas in the city that can serve the modern community as did the Greek *agora* — and from which all vehicle traffic must be excluded — means rediscovering, in its old quarters, the very vitals of the city.

Account must of course be taken of the interests involved, of the circumstances of the inhabitants and their age, of the memories and the factors which bring together and determine certain arrangements and certain preferences in the old town.

If the hub of the old town had above all a social function, rehabilitation must be structural rather than scenographic in purpose.

Civilisation imposed self-discipline, taught men respect and concern for their fellows; we must similarly learn to build and create without destroying in the process all that the past has bequeathed in the way of monuments and art.

4.   EUROPE: THE COMPREHENSIVE EFFORT

François Sorlin

Through the nineteenth century and the first half of the twentieth, the protection and conservation of historic structures were usually limited to the most notable ancient and mediaeval remnants. Other buildings were considered too recent to be worthy of such care which was looked upon as a luxury and as the prerogative of a small number of experts. Legislation and regulations were similarly limited. Monuments were considered separately from their surroundings. Attempts were made to restore ancient structures to what was presumably their original state, but without the help of trustworthy historical and archaeological data. As a result many monuments judged to be of lesser worth were demolished, and areas adjoining such major monuments as Notre Dame in Paris were thoughtlessly razed. Some ruined or decaying monuments were wholly or partially reconstructed, with an abusive reliance on imitative patchwork.

Except in a very few countries (those making up the former Austro-Hungarian Empire appreciated at an early date the value of their old cities), it was only as the result of two world wars — the second in particular — that any notable improvement took place; the extent of the destruction, particularly among the European nations most affected, heightened an awareness both of the monuments and of their urban settings.

After World War II Germany, Italy, Britain, France and Poland totally or partially repaired damage to their historic cities. The new awareness was further accentuated during the last twenty-five years by the rapid pace of social change. This change has gravely prejudiced the artistic and historical heritage, and the danger is increasing with the rapid advance of industrialisation. However, governments now recognise the urgent need of extending the protection once afforded only to individual buildings. This was shown at the World Congress of Architects and Experts of Historical Monuments (in Venice in 1964) and has since been confirmed, *inter alia,* by Unesco, the Council of Europe, and the International Council for Monuments and Sites.

Numerous meetings of experts have defined what is meant by historical groups and sites and their role in society, now and in the future. For too long they have been treated as museum pieces, intended exclusively for aesthetes or tourists. This is now a thing of the past, and we speak today of the integration of groups of buildings and monuments into present-day life, rather than of their conservation.

Any group of buildings may be classified as historical whose homogeneity, and historical, archaeological, aesthetic and picturesque qualities are sufficient to justify preserving it and displaying it to advantage.

This presupposes two factors:

a) The groups must be clearly delimited topographically and architectually, and must constitute a coherent whole, *e.g.* towns and villages set defensively on hills, generally protected by cliffs or ramparts; acropolis-type towns on fortified plateaus; towns on lower ground, also frequently girdled by battlements, or a road which follows the line of the old walls; the historic beginnings of towns that are expanding, usually centred around public buildings (a church or the town hall), with a central square.

If the centre is an important one, it may be enclosed by concentric walls that correspond to consecutive phases of urban growth. In such cases, the whole of the urban fabric enclosed within the outer ring constitutes the historic group, unless the city has undergone such massive alteration or demolition that there are several distinct groupings within the same city.

Homogeneity depends also on the maintenance of the old thoroughfares, and the survival of the original layout and its distribution of masses. It is generally in inverse ratio to the amount of more recent development in the areas concerned.

b) The groups must possess outstanding historical, archaeological or aesthetic qualities. The other qualities which justify preservation and rehabilitation reside less in the character of any single structure than in the quality of the group as a whole. There are nearly always more modest buildings that are collectively important and interesting to the particular group.

The same criteria apply to settings, *e.g.* the square in which a church stands, the village that adjoins a castle; the two together constitute the group. Historical criteria, *e.g.* towns originating in the Middle Ages or at the Renaissance, are in general not too strictly applied, since successive accretions inevitably mark the growth of cities. Geographical or topographical features allow towns to be classified, *e.g.* according to their relation to water (Venice, Bruges, Amsterdam); rural towns, set in the countryside; towns with impressive views of monuments; towns with arcades and old market places; and so on. The characteristic type may vary from country to country, but the idea of historical groups is now well understood and familiar; we can easily identify examples and protect them in such a way as to preserve their fundamental qualities.

Once the general concept has been laid down, the next and most urgent task is to decide what warrants protection (the idea has not yet permeated public consciousness to the extent of creating a demand for an inventory on a world scale).

For over a century, governments have been taking stock and protecting their most important monuments, but seldom showed a similar concern for groups which, accordingly, were often cruelly altered or defaced. In Paris, for example, Haussmann ruthlessly cut new thoroughfares through the heart of the city and destroyed much of its ancient fabric. However experts, metting throughout the world during the last decade, have stressed the need for protective machinery, legal and technical.

Scholarly, exhaustive studies can be made with a view to publication. These are obviously valuable, but may take years, and demand highly-qualified staff. If the need is pressing, something simpler and less cumbersome must be devised, to provide a basis for a national inventory.

One of the best so far available is the Council of Europe cards for the 'Protective Inventory of the European Cultural Heritage (IECH)'. Analytical and descriptive cards of standard dimensions, (21 x 27 cms.), list the following details on the front side:

- geographic location of the city, short description of its history and development;
- present condition: dwellings, public, commercial and industrial activities, and so on;
- prospects for development: housing, tourist, industries, agriculture, cultural activities;
- legal protection available when the card was prepared;
- protective measures proposed in view of the condition of the group, and past or possible future damage;
- short bibliography.

The reverse side of the card allows for the provision of one or two photographs, and a 1 : 10000 plan indicating main features, demarcation lines, and other reference material, *e.g.* city perspectives and restrictions required on height and appearance to preserve the skyline.

Such cards offer two advantages. They permit the identification of cultural property frequently ignored even by the services responsible for their protection, and accordingly even more so by the official or semi-official bodies in charge of development; and they likewise make private owners and local communities aware of the existence and value of such buildings.

In practice, systematic national lists must be made if this information is to be widely known, each historical group having its reference number from its corresponding card. These lists could be arranged in volumes, either geographical (by region, province, department), or by type of group. They should be supplemented with maps, with simple geographical symbols for easy identification of groups. They should be widely distributed, to national, regional and local authorities, the public at large, and societies interested in protection. If it became standard practice to consult them automatically, many of the abusive demolitions that now take place as a result of ignorance or lack of information could be prevented.

Spain, Italy, Malta are among the countries that have started to publish lists, arranged by province; Malta in fact has already completed its catalogue. Britain, Morocco and Tunisia are following their own methods, and often working in co-operation with private agencies. The compiling of such lists constitutes a first step: initial protective measures are taken, and people become aware.

An active rehabilitation policy demands something more elaborate — a rehabilitation inventory which provides the basic data needed to define the potentialities of each historical group and indicating how its revitalisation should be tackled, *i.e.* the basis for a rehabilitation policy.

Generally speaking, public means of protection are no longer adequate. They originated in essentially negative measures that imposed restrictions on architecture, aesthetics and the use made of property (hence the widely-held idea that the owner is cut off from his property in the interests of the community at large). The restrictions are in fact burdensome, especially if the owner receives no tax concessions or subsidies to offset upkeep or improvement costs.

The policy needs changing from passive to active, starting with two sets of measures: tax concessions and financial aid to enable owners to conserve buildings and employ them in character; national, regional and local planning arrangements to ensure historical groups a live role in everyday life. But the obstacles are many.

State action, national and international, must be taken and followed up. Here organisations like Unesco can convince governments of the need for accepted principles and implementing legislation.

The first problem is to convince the services nationally responsible. They are still too often governed by the nineteenth-century idea of items for restoration — completely divorced from their social use and background. This in turn fosters several unfortunate views — that conservationists are narrow-minded conservatives, that historical groups are lifeless and useless and merely hold up social development. We should, instead, look upon conservation not as an end in itself but as another means of returning cultural values to their proper place in our own society.

The problem is not only archaeological or architectural, but one to be taken into account in regional development and social and economic expansion.

Legislation can be considered under three main headings: safeguarding; town planning; and rehabilitation.

a) Safeguarding

Some States now have laws which recognise the status of historical groups as such; this in itself is a marked advance.

Netherlands

The definition in the 1961 Act on cultural heritage is 'Any group of immovable objects (such as roads, streets, squares, bridges, canals, waterways) which, in conjunction with one or more monuments in the group, forms a scene which is of public interest in that it lends beauty or character to the whole'.

Article 15 of the same Act lays down the procedure to be followed: 'After consultation with the Monuments Council, the Municipal Council, the Provincial Executive Council and the Permanent Commission for Regional Development, the Ministers of Culture and Housing shall be empowered to designate the towns or villages to be protected. The Minister's decision shall be published in the Official Journal of the Netherlands and communicated to the councils concerned.'

The municipal authorities are then bound to take the necessary measures, and to adapt their regulations accordingly. Should they fail to do so within the allotted time (one or two years), the provincial government is empowered to act in their stead. The central government and the provincial government are also entitled to comment on the plans and regulations. The various decisions are entered in a register which is open to public scrutiny.

Italy

The Act of 6th August 1967 extends the 1942 legislation by provisions covering 'protected areas' in towns which 'are of artistic or historical interest, or have exceptional surroundings, including the immediate neighbourhood, which may be considered as an integral part of the towns themselves'.

Various parameters are used to demarcate these zones: surveys of districts in which most blocks contain pre-1860 buildings 'even in the absence of monuments or buildings of major artistic value'; 'ancient walls preserved in whole or in part'; 'an urban area which constitutes an outstanding example of municipal planning'.

Under a new general Act that will consolidate and replace certain Acts passed in 1939 no action can be taken on property, in the absence of a town planning scheme, which is declared to be of cultural value in its environment until a development plan or construction programme has been established in agreement with the Superintendance of Monuments, and approved; the Superintendent is responsible for ensuring that the outline programme laid down by the Regional Commission is respected.

If the municipality fails to act, the higher authority — as in the Netherlands — can intervene and appoint a Commissioner who acts in lieu and draws up the plans. Works affecting the general appearance of the surroundings, the conservation or restoration of existing structures and any alterations to them must be carried out under the supervision of the Superintendent of Monuments.

Such provisions, legally establishing the concept of historical groups and surveillance over them, had no equivalent in earlier legislation.

However, the accent is more on coercion than persuasion. There is little encouragement to communities or owners to take the initiative; economic development, tax concessions and financial assistance all depend on direct intervention by the public authority.

b) Town Planning

Britain

The Civic Amenities Act was passed in Britain in 1967. It stipulates that all local planning authorities (county and county borough councils) must designate urban areas of architectural or historical interest within their jurisdiction as conservation areas. The Ministers, local planning authorities, and any other bodies involved are then obliged, in accordance with the Town and Country Planning Acts, and the Ancient Monuments Act 1953, to ensure the maintenance of the general fabric and principal features of such areas.

The local authorities can compulsorily purchase and, if necessary, subsequently sell any building registered as being of outstanding historical or architectural interest, particularly if the owner is not taking adequate measures to safeguard it. They may also take possession of the property and themselves carry out the necessary repairs.

Some 1 200 areas have been designated, 420 as being of outstanding historical or architectural interest; four cities of major importance (Bath, Chester, Chichester and York) were selected for pilot experiments in evaluating the cost of safeguarding old towns — which parts require urgent repairs, and the cost.

State subsidies under the Ancient Monuments Act to assist owners to maintain old buildings located in historic cities amount to £700,000 annually. The State contributes 25 per cent, the municipality 25, and the owner the remaining 50. This aid is not limited to conservation areas, but can extend to town schemes in the four pilot cities, and to individual buildings in modern towns.

Sweden
The Old City of Stockholm Act (Lex Gamla Stan) 1963, was passed to 'safeguard the buildings of the old city, with due regard to the technical and functional considerations involved', *i.e.* to preserve the character and atmosphere of the old town while modernising the dwellings and adapting them to modern needs.

The municipality buys the sites, and rents the buildings on long-term leases which stipulate that the building must be used for the purpose for which it was restored. The price paid for the site enables the owner to defray the cost of restoring and modernising his property.

The ground rent charged is quite low — in some cases, no rent at all is payable during the first ten years. The restoration is thus practically an interest-free investment which the owner has ample time to write off.

Such arrangements, however, are feasible only in countries where the political and legislative system fosters collective ownership of the land, as in Sweden and some Nordic countries. In view of the increasing involvement of public authorities with private property, they offer an example which could with advantage be followed elsewhere.

c) Rehabilitation

France
Of special interest is the Malraux Act 1962 in France. It appears to be the only legislation that aims at dealing simultaneously with all the problems — technical, economic, social and financial — involved in the rehabilitation of historic groups.

The basic principle is that rehabilitation should not depend solely on the resources available to the Minister responsible for the cultural heritage, but be the joint concern also of the Ministry of Public Works and Housing, and of the local authorities and local people involved. As a descriptive term 'safeguarded areas' is rather too passive, and should be dropped in favour of 'revitalised' or 'rehabilitated' areas.

These areas are defined and designated in common by both Ministers; the decision becomes effective only after consultation, and with the consent of the local communities. In theory, the designation can be made by the central authority; in practice, every effort is made to obtain the consent and support of the local authorities, without which any rehabilitation has little chance of success. The result has sometimes been to restrict the size of the area, which then serves as an example that encourages the municipality to ask itself that the area be extended, to take in, say, the whole of an old town.

72

Conservation applies for a period of two years in the protected area immediately it is designated, so as to prevent speculators from breaking up or dismembering buildings.

During the two years a safeguard and rehabilitation plan is prepared in two parts which are complementary and closely connected.

1. The architectural restoration. An analysis is made, detailing the state and the interest of the individual buildings, which should be pulled down, new buildings to be erected, sites to be cleared, items to be put to new uses. An architectural schedule is then prepared, indicating, for each building, restoration or reconstruction measures to be taken, materials to be used, size and scale of new structures, courtyards and gardens to be provided or improved.

The work is carried out by the Ministry of Cultural Affairs. Plans cover different categories of buildings.

i) Historic monuments included in groups. Under the Malraux Act all the existing provisions regarding restoration (Law of 31st December 1913) remain valid — protected monuments should obviously not receive less favourable treatment than more modest buildings included in a rehabilitation project, *e.g.* it would hardly make sense to restore the Marais in Paris without restoring the Place des Vosges, which forms part of it. Such problems, with their legal and financial implications, must be solved by the services responsible for the conservation of monuments in co-ordination with the bodies implementing the restoration project.

ii) Buildings which, though not classified, are wholly or partially of substantial archaeological or artistic interest. So far as possible, these should be treated like monuments, with particular care to their architectural and internal and external features.

iii) Minor buildings which provide the connecting tissue of the group. Separately, they are not monuments, but do collectively contribute something distinctive. Here the foreman in charge is allowed somewhat more freedom, but must nevertheless respect the directions regarding appearance, colours, openings, materials and slope of roofs specified in the architectural schedule.

Should some houses be dilapidated beyond hope of repair, or likely to contribute little to the restoration, the plan specifies whether or not they should be replaced by new buildings that will fit in satisfactorily.

2. The detailed town planning scheme. Drawn up at the same time as the architectural restoration plan, this is based on an analysis of the city or neighbourhood. It is part of the general development plan for the city and area and shows what measures are necessary

The Hotel Sully (before and after restoration)

specifically for the remodelled historical group *(iii)* (thoroughfares, access, equipment, sanitation). To ensure coherent planning, the study is made under the responsibility of the Ministry for Public Works and Housing by the team which prepares the architectural restoration plan.

Special attention is paid to two points.

i) Defining the new functions of the historical group. Can the group again fulfil its original purpose or serve for something else which does not alter or distort its character? There would be little point in drawing up rules for conserving buildings which serve no social purpose — indeed, one of the basic concerns of the Malraux Act is to define a role for groups rehabilitated.

Article 13 of the implementing decree of 13th July 1963 expressly stipulates that the permanent protection and rehabilitation plan shall replace and supersede any existing limited town planning schemes. Certain regulations regarding alignments, for instance, that were applied to some extent in the nineteenth and early twentieth centuries are now obsolete, and cannot be invoked to justify demolitions once the plan has been approved.

Clearly, only a detailed study of the urban fabric and its composition can indicate what each building within the group was intended for; hence the analysis carried out under the Act will be necessarily long and complex, and takes a minimum of two years.

ii) The group and the new city. Sanitation, and traffic and parking, raise complex legal and administrative problems which, as indicated in the Malraux Act, must be solved through a detailed plan which has the force of law.

To maintain the ancient fabric, the plan has to say where the main and subsidiary traffic will pass, and decide the relations of mass and scale between the city's original core and its new outgrowths (particularly if, as often happens, the old city is surrounded by walls, and growth can only take place outside).

The aim of the French experiment is thus, in old cities, to reconcile revitalisation with preservation; and the consent and support of both the local authorities and the local inhabitants is vital.

Generous provision is accordingly made for consultation at every stage: when the area is initially selected and demarcated; then, at every phase as the plan is elaborated there is a survey of public opinion, and the mayors attend the meetings of the national commission for safeguarded areas which considers and if necessary amends the proposals of the architects and town planners.

Financial provisions of the Malraux Act. Under the Act, two kinds of cleaning up and modernisation projects can be financed, in accordance with the regulations concerning urban renewal.

a) projects to preserve, restore and improve protected areas;

b) projects to rehabilitate buildings, including reconditioning, modernisation or demolition, to improve living conditions within a group of buildings, providing that these operations are carried out within the zoning limits established by the Minister for Public Works and Housing, after a public inquiry and with the approval of the community or communities concerned.

Projects of type *(a)* are practically the only ones used in France to revitalise historical groups. The municipality sets up a semi-public company to carry out the plan. It includes representatives of the local communities, banks, chambers of commerce, owners of buildings and representatives of the State, and is responsible for the execution, in successive stages, for restoring the buildings and modernising the dwellings.
One or many operational units are selected within the protected area because of their outstanding historical or architectural interest and the social circumstances in the town or area concerned. The latter condition is vital: works which entail moving out large numbers of people cause extreme discontent and this could easily compromise the whole rehabilitation scheme; arrangements must be made beforehand to accommodate elsewhere any people who must be moved out while the work is in progress.

The semi-public company acts for the owners. If they agree, it can make a partnership arrangement with them, under which they return to their houses as soon as the work is completed, and pay an agreed share of the cost. Otherwise, the building is purchased, either under an amicable arrangement or through expropriation. The restored building is then either sold, once the work is completed (the former owner having first call), or rented (with due regard to the appreciated value resulting from the modernisation).

The semi-public company is financed via State subsidies and loans from credit agencies. The operation is thus financially stable from the outset. Medium and long-term loans are made to the owners, who must contribute their share (20 − 30 per cent) of the total outlay.

Fifteen such operational units have been set up in the forty areas (2,100 hectares) designated to date. The area of the units is still limited, as the funds earmarked for urban renewal are rather scarce. Cities affected include Paris, Lyon, Chartres, Colmar, Avignon, Bourges, Poitiers, Sarlat, Rouen, Uzès.

The principles established by Malraux Act seem satisfactory, but their effectiveness is limited because the subsidies granted by the State are far from being commensurate with needs. Consequently, there is a trend towards making greater use of a provision in Article 3 of

An old mansion in the Marais after restoration

the Act stipulating that owners may form associations to carry out the works proposed in the rehabilitation plan. Future progress undoubtedly depends on private initiative on a large scale; the public sector cannot reasonably be expected to take sole responsibility for conserving and revitalising old quarters and cities.

This is also the only way in which people themselves will come to realise their own responsibility in regard to their cultural heritage. It is important to eliminate a certain feeling that it does not really concern them, which at present seriously limits the practical effects of the Act.

International attention to Groups

Some new conclusions can be drawn from the legislative and administrative experience of States.

First, the historical group concept is now familiar to the public and increasingly reflected in national legislation.

The public awareness, which now seems firmly established and unlikely to disappear again, is reflected in a number of international measures adopted or under consideration.

In the draft convention for the protection of the world cultural and natural heritage, for example, Unesco attaches great importance to the problems of groups, their conservation and improvement.

Similarly, the European Ministers of Culture, meeting in Brussels in November 1969 under the auspices of the Council of Europe, decided henceforth to co-ordinate on a permanent basis with their ministerial colleagues responsible for urbanism and development. They proposed to hold regular joint meetings, and to set up a committee of governmental experts to examine recommendations made to States to bring their legislation into line with the new principles. In future, the basis of such legislation should be planning at all levels — national, regional and local. Cultural values (including those embodied in historical groups) must find their proper place in town-planning schemes and so on in this aspect of contemporary civilisation.

The fabric of our old cities has often been gravely and even disastrously impaired owing to the enforcement of outdated regulations, or simply because of a lack of liaison between planners and those responsible for the protection of the cultural heritage. These cities represent an enormous housing capital and potential but are still often treated as if they were irrelevant to social and economic development — if not positive obstacles in its way.

This is a problem of political awareness and of administrative practice. We have seen that the legislation and regulations of most

Excavations in the square of Notre Dame Cathedral, Paris

States are no longer adequate.

The first change necessary in the law is to change the concept of conservation from passive to active. This presupposes that, in compensation for the legitimate restrictions they impose, the public authorities substantially aid owners, through enough tax concessions and subsidies to cover the cost of conserving groups that are worth preserving.

This implies far reaching administrative changes, governmental policy decisions, and interministerial legislation; for the means at the disposal of the ministers responsible for the cultural heritage are nearly everywhere too limited for an effective rehabilitation policy for old cities.

Funds must be drawn on amounts earmarked for housing; indeed, priority could sometimes be accorded, even on the specific grounds of housing improvement, to the restoration and renovation of buildings that make up historical centres.

Plans for the use of this capital wealth — the buildings — should be drawn up jointly by the various departments involved, in close co-operation with the regional and local authorities.

New legislation and regulations of this kind are at present under study in many countries. There is reason to hope that, with the active encouragement of Unesco and of the great regional organisations such as the Council of Europe, we may soon see major improvements.

The excessive rise in the price of land in urban areas is a major (if indirect) cause of the deterioration of old buildings. To prevent speculation, the price of land must be controlled in urban zones that are potential urban renovation areas. Systematic control has already weaned promoters in many countries from destruction and persuaded them of the validity of remodelling as an alternative. But this demands the enforcement, at the same time, of very strict town-planning regulations.

The effectiveness of governmental action can be greatly enhanced if consistently supported by the local authorities — whose powers of decision tend constantly to increase. If channelled towards the assertion and maintenance of a traditional way of life, the influence of elected local representatives may be decisive. It is absolutely essential to have their support.

5. THE UNITED STATES: FEDERAL FUNDS FOR RESCUE

Christopher Tunnard

Although cities in the continental United States date only from the last half of the sixteenth century (St Augustine, Florida was founded by Spain in 1565), and they remained small throughout the seventeenth and eighteenth centuries, their fabric abounds in interest for the social and architectural historian. A belated glance is now being given by American society as a whole which, in this generation, has become acutely conscious of urban problems. In spite of the frequent fires which still plague the older sections, and regardless of neglect, blight, decay and demolition, much remains to remind us of a cultural history very different from that of our own day.

A restoration has been in progress at St Augustine for the last ten years. The principal agency involved is the St Augustine Historical and Preservation Commission, established by the State of Florida, which prepared a master plan in 1960 and has since been engaged in construction and fund-raising. A separate non-profit educational corporation, St Augustine Restoration, Inc., was established to receive gifts and undertake restoration of the old quarter. A sustained effort has been made by this group to generate interest in the old city as a centre of Hispano-American culture.

The majority of the old quarters of American cities are products of the nineteenth century. Although isolated examples of earlier periods abound, it is rare to find a whole district of eighteenth-century vintage, except in specialised circumstances like the Moravian village of Old Salem, North Carolina or the Colonial sea-port of Newport, Rhode Island. There were very few cities of importance in the pre-Revolutionary period, while in Virginia there had been in the beginning a positive aversion to founding towns on the part of the plantation owners, who preferred to control the shipment of maize and tobacco from their own docks along the rivers. But since the history of the Colonial period has great fascination for Americans, numerous examples of seventeenth- and eighteenth-century reconstruction have appeared in attempts to make up for this lack, while still-standing examples of Greek Revival and other periods have been allowed to fall into ruin. Examples of such reconstruction are the Pioneer Village of Salem, Massachusetts, a well-researched outdoor museum of the primitive shelters invented by the first settlers, and Plymouth Plantation, a reconstruction of the main street of early Plymouth, Massachusetts on a new site, with a reproduction of the ship Mayflower at anchor in a lagoon nearby.

Unfortunately, the remaining Colonial houses are not always safe from demolition by public and private interests, whose ideas do not always coincide with those of the preservationist. Preservation by law is a comparatively recent phenomenon in the United States, which has always carefully guarded the constitutional rights of property owners, even in many cases against the demands of the State itself.

If the bulk of old quarters in American cities is thus found to be nineteenth century in date, this does not mean that they are devoid of architectural or historic interest. That century encompassed a host of styles, and coincided with the rise of urbanisation generally. Americans were prodigious town builders in those years, and although foreigners are perhaps more fascinated by tales of cowboys on empty plains, the mercantile city, followed by its industrial counterpart, spread westward with great rapidity from 1800 onwards, tempering the myth of Eldorado with the more sober pursuits of earning a living in the mill and the counting house. Schools, newspapers, libraries and theatres could be found in the cities of Cincinnati on the Ohio and St Louis on the Mississippi River as early as the 1820s. Exclusive residential districts were formed early — one of the special characteristics of the American city being the separation of the work-place from the home, a feature which marked a frontier city like Pittsburgh.[1] Whereas industrial growth in Stoke-on-Trent in England, for example, mixed terrace houses with the pottery kilns in a seemingly haphazard manner, American cities tended to have residential districts clearly marked; and while industries sometimes penetrated them, their separateness has helped to give them an identity which makes preservation more logical and rewarding.

These residential districts are quite often found close to the old heart of the town and, in our own day, have been vulnerable to forces other than industrial. No longer fashionable, as the population has moved away to the suburbs, they have acquired secondary uses that are not always well-adapted. Divided and subdivided, such buildings have often survived only by the quality of their construction or workmanship.

Further out from the centre of the modern city one may come across other old sections, where once, perhaps there was an industrial village, which has now been absorbed in the lateral expansion of the metropolis. These villages often had interesting architecture. A well-known example of the type is Pullman, Illinois (where the Palace Railroad Car was manufactured), which has a place in the history of the American labour movement.[2] It is now part of Chicago. Further out again from this city is another type, the suburban community of Riverside, Illinois, planned in the picturesque manner by Olmsted and

82

Vaux in 1868. In 1970 it was awarded the status of a national historic landmark by the Federal Government.

Apart from the cities there are historic towns, many of which are protected in some way or have been the subject of partial restoration. Typical of these are the silver mining towns of Colorado, now abandoned, each with its 'opera house' and main street of 'false front' architecture, and the Gold Rush towns of California, a good example of which is Columbia, a town having in 1853 it is said 143 faro games, four banks, thirty saloons, three express offices, a stadium for bear and bull fights, a theatre and a brewery; all these, and California's first schoolhouse, were built in red brick. Twelve square blocks of Columbia have been preserved and restored as part of the State park system.

There are also charming courthouse towns of the South and Middle West, the village greens of New England, mill villages and religious utopias. Some of the latter, *e.g.* the Amana villages in Iowa, are still flourishing entities. There are river towns, lake and sea ports, lumber towns, head-of-navigation towns and many other types, each with its different institutions and interesting ethnic differences. Sometimes, also, a famous architect has left an indelible impression on a town, like Henry Hobson Richardson, the inventor of the Richardsonian Romanesque style, in North Easton, Massachusetts or Frank Lloyd Wright on Oak Park, Illinois.

If the old districts vary in architectural style, they are also marked by a difference in materials. Boston, Philadelphia and Charleston, South Carolina have street after street of red brick, while New York was invaded after 1850 by the chocolate-coloured brownstone which was used for its town houses, built in rows or terraces, a fashion which quickly spread to other cities. But wood frame and stucco were also used, and many of the important older houses are of post-and-lintel construction. After the balloon frame method of construction was invented in 1833, urban houses continued to be built in wood, as San Francisco and other western cities bear witness, until the fire-laws made masonry construction compulsory in cities. The first tenement building of large size was built in New York in 1850, and even these, although until recently not thought worthy, are now being reconditioned for apartment house use in the current shortage. Cast-iron warehouses have proved to be excellent subjects for preservation. Unfortunately, in St Louis and other cities, whole districts of this type of construction were torn down before historians of technology had pointed out their importance in the American cultural heritage. New York City has recently preserved several office buildings of this type, and is now faced with the far more difficult task of preserving early skyscrapers like the famous Woolworth Building completed in 1913, a steel-frame tower by the architect

Cass Gilbert with many original features of construction and
decoration.

Growth of Interest in Historic Preservation

'In America', wrote the Boston antiquarian William Summer Appleton
in 1913 to potential members of his Society for the Preservation of
New England Antiquities, 'unlike Europe, respect for and interest in
antiquities is considered more an individual then a State duty'.[3] The
beginnings of historic preservation in the United States are thus to be
identified with private interests. Rescuing a building here and there
was for long the prerogative of dedicated individuals like Appleton, or
of local historical societies. The latter seldom rescued more than one
house, he complained. It was then usually used as a historic house
museum. These museums are opened to the public and kept in operation
by entrance fees and private subscriptions; this continues to provide an
important means of preservation. While in 1895 only twenty historic
house museums could be counted in the entire country, today there
are over a thousand.

In its early days this movement reflected the ideas of the moment in
restoration, which was frequently inaccurate or insufficiently informed.
Measured drawings were not in general use until well into the present
century, when architects began to take an interest in the American past
as well as in the European. They were spurred on by the influential
architectural firm of McKim, Mead and White, whose three famous
partners made a journey through New England in 1876 to study and
make drawings of 'the best examples of Colonial work'.

Undoubtedly the most important of nineteenth-century efforts to
save Colonial buildings was the banding together of a group of ladies
in the 1850s to save Mount Vernon, the site of Washington's house and
tomb, when the State of Virginia and the Federal Government had
refused to pay the asking price. The house and grounds remain in the
hands of the Mount Vernon Ladies' Association of the Union
(chartered in 1856) and nowadays receive over a million visitors
a year.

Thus, while the Federal Government had long been interested in
preserving sites of scenic and natural beauty (the centennial of
Yellowstone National Park, the first of its kind, fell in 1972), it was
not until the early 1900s that the nation was forced to consider
the necessity of preserving antiquities. The first such action was the
passing of the Antiquities Act under President Theodore Roosevelt,
in 1906. The informed public had become alarmed at the destruction
of Indian artifacts in the south-west, and the new legislation enabled
the President to proclaim national monuments on certain land.

84

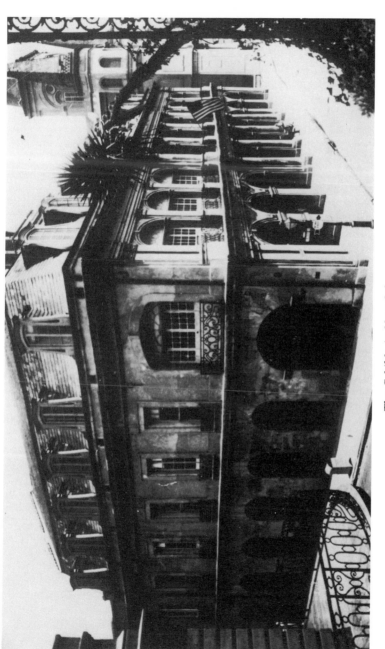

The Cabildo in New Orleans

Often the Indian sites were in national parks or reservations. The archaeological finds thus preserved were to be displayed in public museums.

After this first step, and apart from the formation of the National Park Service in 1916, the country had to wait until 1935 and the administration of President Franklin D. Roosevelt for the passage of the Historic Sites Act, which brought all Federal preservation under the control of the Park Service. This new agency of government had been preserving famous battlefields and other historic sites; now it was empowered to own, operate and restore historic buildings and improve their surroundings. Some of these were in the cities, such as the compound containing the old Custom House, the Derby mansion and the Derby wharf in Salem, Massachusetts, an early settlement which had a second lease of life in the American China Trade.

Meanwhile other important events had taken place in the late 1920s and early 1930s. The first of these was the example set by John D. Rockefeller, Jr. in the rescue of an entire Colonial town. This was Williamsburg, Virginia. Rockefeller started buying up properties in 1927 and formed a holding company, Williamsburg Restoration, Inc., which undertook to restore and reconstruct the town to its former appearance as the State capital of Virginia. Resident historians and architects were kept busy authenticating the work and reviving the ancient crafts like candle-making and glass-blowing. Even the bricks were made from local clay.

The key to the importance of Williamsburg is 'interpretation'. Rather than let the restored town houses, courthouses, mansions and jails speak for themselves, the corporation encourages an enormous educational effort. Besides the accommodation of thousands of visitors who are guided through the buildings by costumed interpreters of this replica of Colonial life, a constant stream of books, furniture reproductions, arts and crafts and, latterly, movies, on aspects of the Colonial world pour out of the city. Week-long seminars are held annually on antiques, gardens and folk art. Visiting European dignitaries are often brought there for a day or two on their arrival in the United States before taking up the strenuous round of official visits in nearby Washington. It is the role of Williamsburg to show the nation and the world an American culture not to be found in the hustle and bustle of the modern American way of life. After Williamsburg showed the way, 'interpretation' of historic properties became quite common.

Williamsburg does not suffer from lack of funds. (An endowment fund of some $50 million, nearly all of it provided by Mr Rockefeller, ensures that any operating deficit beyond the returns from sales and tourists can be made up out of income.) It is unique in this respect, and preservation of a whole city or a district has usually to be undertaken by other means. It was in 1931 that a group of interested citizens and public officials passed the first historic zoning ordinance in the United States in Charleston, South Carolina. Among other restraints, this ordinance controls exterior architectural features. But more action was needed, and the Historic Charleston Foundation was formed to acquire funds to buy up old houses and resell them to new owners under a restrictive covenant. The two measures together have made the historic districts of Charleston, a town first settled in the early eighteenth century, into a first-class tourist attraction.

The Vieux Carré Commission in New Orleans was established in 1937. This is a public body which exercises control over important details like wrought-iron balconies and fanlights in the old French Quarter. New building is strictly controlled and 'demolition by neglect' (or calculated ruin by recalcitrant owners) forbidden. Prominent citizens are numbered among the commissioners.

It will be seen that although public and private preservation efforts have often gone hand in hand (and sometimes in forced marriages) the larger task has until recently remained in the private sector — almost 70 per cent of all preservation activity, according to some authorities. To co-ordinate and assist this array of private interests, the National Trust for Historic Preservation was formed in 1949, with federal enabling legislation signed by President Truman, but independent of government. Like its prototype in Britain, the Trust was empowered to receive properties as well as to help individuals and groups in preservation methods and tactics. Over the years the Trust has been active in providing information and acting as an agent between government and citizen. It was the Trust, too, which promoted the idea of preserving buildings in their context, causing a second series of historic zones all over the country — charming brick streets of houses like Georgetown in Washington and Beacon Hill in Boston, the latter made possible by an act of the Massachusetts State Legislature in 1955.

Federal Activities

Finally, in 1966, a broadening of the machinery of the Federal Government made its leadership possible by the passage of the Historic Preservation Act in the administration of President Johnson. Most importantly, funds were authorised for preservation action in the entire country, $32 million being the initial sum specified. Several other provisions were made in the Housing Act of 1966 and other Acts of Congress which aid preservation. The most important of these will be described.

Whereas in Europe, Latin America of Asia historic preservation may come under a Ministry of Culture or of Fine Arts, the National Park Service remains the chief administrative body under the Historic Preservation Act, which provides matching grants to the States and also money for the support of the National Trust. The National Register is enlarged to include State and locally significant buildings. Under Section 106 of the Act, the heads of federal agencies and departments must take into account the effect of federal, federally assisted or federally licensed projects on National Register properties. If affected, the case must be presented for comment to the Advisory Council for Historic Preservation. State-wide historic surveys are initiated with federal help and financial assistance is made to individual restoration projects. An Office of Archaeology and Historic Preservation provides documentation and screens projects.

The Advisory Council on Historic Preservation consists of seventeen members, ten of whom are private citizens. The others are heads of various departments of government. Its function under Section 106 of the 1966 Act is exemplified in the discussion of the case of Vieux Carré, New Orleans, discussed later in this Chapter.

Some minor programmes:
1. The Federal Inter-Agency Salvage Program is concerned with the stabilisation of ruins, and archaeological salvage. It was made necessary in 1945 by the construction of dams by the United States Army Corps of Engineers and the Bureau of Reclamation.
2. The Surplus Property Act of 1944 gives an opportunity for others to acquire federal properties to be disposed of by the General Services Administration. Over fifty historic properties have been transferred in this way.
3. The Land and Water Conservation Fund Act of 1965 provides grants in aid to the States that may include historic and cultural sites. Recreation is usually stressed. An example of funding can be seen in the Governor Paca Gardens and Visitor Interpretation Center in Anapolis, Maryland, where William Paca, who was a signatory of the Declaration of Independence, built his magnificent house in 1763 in the traditional five-part plan of the Maryland mansions of his day. The gardens are now being restored..
4. The Economic Development Administration, which includes tourist development among its activities, has aided in the restoration of an entire Shaker village at Lexington, Kentucky; the reconditioning of an old canal at Rome, New York for recreational purposes; and has financed a survey of St Genevieve, Missouri (a town noted for the French influence on its architecture), to help establish it as a tourist attraction.

The Department of Housing and Urban Development

This Department — HUD as it is usually called — has the greatest potential for the revitalisation of historic quarters at federal level.

Coincidental with the national interest in the deterioration of the American city, an interest which roughly dates from the end of World War II, the Federal Government's activities in housing gradually changed from individual projects to the renewal of whole districts, including the economically threatened commercial centres. The latter type of renewal was especially favoured by city mayors, who saw their shopping streets decaying with the move of retailing to the less congested suburbs.

One of the most spectacular examples of urban renewal tied to historic preservation is to be found in Society Hill, Philadelphia, where there was a good housing stock of brick construction. In twenty-five square blocks Society Hill contains hundreds of residential buildings of historic and architectural importance dating back to the Colonial period. Independence Hall is nearby. Private efforts were made in the 1930s and 1940s to preserve the area, but government help was needed to make it habitable — schools, parks, parking, walkways, and a food distribution centre to replace the old market were needed. Work started in 1956, and by 1972 almost 700 old houses have been or were being restored, many with a fair degree of historical accuracy. Some were reconditioned by their owners, others were acquired by the Redevelopment Authority which controlled the exterior appearance and sold them to a non-profit corporation which in turn found new owners.

While some authorities consider that too many fine houses were removed in the process of renewal and that three new apartment house towers included in the renewal scheme spoil a skyline formerly dominated by the graceful spires of Colonial churches, Society Hill exhibits ingenious examples of adaptive use and a control of the environment which has cleared it of accumulated debris and blight. It also contains a mixture of income groups not too different from that of its earlier prosperous existence — tradesmen, merchants, wealthy burghers and office clerks.

At the time of renewal in Society Hill, no federal funds were available for the primary purpose of restoring buildings to authentic historical conditions. These funds could be spent for enhancing and protecting the surroundings and removing blighting influences, for planning and some other aids, but not for restoration. Home improvement loans helped somewhat but not enough. This lacuna was corrected in the Demonstration Cities Act of 1966, some five years after the term 'historic' had first been mentioned in the housing Acts (Housing Act of 1961). The 1966 Act specifically designated 'preservation activities and planning as eligible project costs'. One million dollars was appropriated for this purpose in the first year of the Act's operation and fifteen matching grants were made. This has since increased to forty-six grants with a cumulative total of $2,822,414 expended. Buildings saved and restored under this programme include a South San Francisco Opera House of the 1880s, the painter Thomas Eakins' house and studio in Philadelphia (to be used as a museum and art centre), a half-timbered house in Helena, Montana, reminiscent of European building techniques, the magnificent Shirley-Eustis house in Roxbury, Massachusetts, a New England Academy in Haverhill, Massachusetts (where the poet John Greenleaf Whittier went to school), a century-old Hawaiian church, and several others. Communities are encouraged to use the restored buildings for such purposes as civic offices and community centres. Projects must be in an urban setting and consistent with the local comprehensive plan. All properties assisted must meet the criteria of the National Register of Historic Places.

This new responsibility on the part of the Department of Housing and Urban Development, under whose earlier programmes local authorities had sometimes destroyed much significant architecture, was epitomised by its Secretary, George Romney: 'A city without a sense of its past can have little hope of planning for its future. For cities, like people, the heritage of the past can provide the identity and the place around which new commitments are made.'

The Department of Transportation
In the year 1966, in which so much important legislation affecting preservation was enacted, a measure creating a Department of Transporation was passed. Under this Department comes the Federal Highway Administration and the Bureau of Public Roads, which have great impact on the revitalisation of old neighbourhoods. To avoid or minimise harm, the Administrator must consider alternate plans when a district is threatened by a new highway. Two public hearings are now required before a highway using federal funds is built.

There are various reasons for this. The States have their own highway departments which carry out the federally-aided inter-State highway programme begun in 1956 and not yet finished. These State departments use the power of eminent domain to acquire property in the cities served by the inter-State network. The State highway departments have not been notable for preserving old quarters and have seldom even made an effort to document historic values. They have provided numerous examples of intrusion of public works on scenic or historic areas. They are now required to relocate the dispossessed, but marginal businesses have proved significantly difficult to re-establish elsewhere than in the older parts of the city where the shop or business was originally established. Both housing and commerce have sometimes suffered by the taking of land under this programme.

An example of action under the new legislation, involving the Department of Transportation, the Louisiana State Highway Department, the Advisory Council on Historic Preservation and numerous citizen groups is given below, in much abbreviated form. It shows that a highway need not actually destroy an old quarter physically in order to do irreparable harm to its existence.

Resolution of a Conflict: A Case Study

The Historic Preservation Act (Public Law 89-665) affords an element of protection for districts, sites, buildings, structures, and objects in the National Register under the provisions of Section 106:

> 'The head of any federal agency having direct or indirect jurisdiction over a proposed federal or federally assisted undertaking in any State and the head of any federal department or independent agency shall, prior to the issuance of any license, as the case may be, take into account the effect of the undertaking on any district, site, building, structure, or object that is included in the National Register. The head of any such federal agency shall afford the Advisory Council on Historic Preservation established under title II of this Act a reasonable opportunity to comment with regard to such undertaking.'

The Advisory Council mentioned is composed partly of heads of departments or agencies of government and partly of private citizens, of which the writer was one for a two-year term ending in 1969. When the Council votes, the department heads concerned are a party to the recommendations made.

An important case invoking Section 106 of the Historic Preservation Act was that of the proposed Inter-State Route 310 (the Riverfront-Eylsian Fields Expressway) affecting the Vieux Carré in New Orleans, one of the country's first historic districts and in 1965 designated as a National Historic Site in the National Register.

The National Register's description of the revitalised district is expressed as follows:

> 'The Vieux Carré has evolved over a long period of time. It was begun in 1718 on a site selected by de Bienville on the east bank of the Mississippi River, but in a great bend which makes the site lie west of the river. The town was laid out in a typical early

New Orleans, French Quarter: 'Iron Lace'

eighteenth-century French grid pattern with 300-foot square blocks. In the centre of the town next to the river a parade ground evolved surrounded by those government and church structures which today constitute Jackson Square. The accepted boundaries of the Vieux Carré today are the river, Canal Street, North Rampart Street, and the Esplanade Avenue. In the early eighteenth century these streets ran along the top of the protective leveés to prevent flooding of the town and were later marked by fortifications.

The town grew as a centre of commerce due to its strategic importance so close to the mouth of the Mississippi, but events elsewhere overshadowed its growing importance. The end of the French and Indian War, or the Seven Years War as it was known in Europe, forced the French to cede their territory to the British and Spanish. Spain took possession of the Louisiana Territory, including New Orleans, in 1762 but it was 1768 before a Spanish government was firmly established. Changes in the structures in the Vieux Carré took place during attempts to fortify the town during the war and by the Spanish after they took possession. In 1788, a disastrous fire swept through the city and destroyed, according to the Governor's account, "Eight hundred and fifty-six buildings..." including many public and parochial structures. No sooner was the town rebuilt than another fire of equal proportions occurred in 1792. New building regulations were then posted requiring the use of brick or the covering of wooden frames with a thick layer of plaster. At the same time, the old French fortifications around the town were rebuilt.

In 1800, Napoleon reclaimed the Louisiana Territory from Spain, but fearing loss to the English, he sold it to the United States in 1803. One of the first changes made by the Americans was the removal of the fort surrounding the town (which by this time spilled outside the walls anyway) and its conversion to broad, tree-lined boulevards.

Until about 1850, the Vieux Carré went through a period of alternate restoration and new commercial development, the latter primarily confined to the waterfront where the river was adding alluvium to the shoreline. After 1850, there was an upsurge in the activity of commercial development, most of which took place outside the limits of the Vieux Carré. The shift of commerce away from the area led to a gradual decline and a shift in populations, and by the end of the nineteenth century the area was already considered as a curiosity and attracting tourists. One facet of the commercial development did significantly change the character of the area, however. In 1867, the railroad was extended along the shorelines levée and with it came the warehouses which choked off the view of the river from Jackson Square. These warehouses have only recently been removed. Twentieth-century developments in the area have included the destruction of a few old landmarks and the incursion of more modern buildings in place of older ones. The increase of a new industry in tourism has led to the building in recent years of facilities to house and feed these visitors within the confines of the Vieux Carré.

In summary, the Vieux Carré does not reflect any one segment of American history so much as it shows the development of that history in a restricted area. There exists a range of structures from the early French to the modern period, and this reflects the fact that each generation builds on the foundations laid down by the preceding ones and assimilates its own innovations with its inheritance.'

A new highway facility had been suggested for the riverfront of New Orleans for many years. In 1944 Robert Moses made a specific recommendation. As the Bureau of Public Roads put it:

'For several years plans have been made to place Inter-State 310 along the river side of the Vieux Carré for the purpose of relieving traffic congestion in the Quarter, a project largely to be funded with federal monies. Due to the controversy which has raged over this project several alternatives have been proposed for the design of the road to take into account the historic setting upon which it will intrude.'

The National Register's interest
On 21 December 1965, Secretary of the Interior Udall declared the Vieux Carré eligible for designation as a National Historic Landmark because of its national significance in American history and architecture. The district was automatically included in the National Register of Historic Places and with the passage of the National Register of Historic Preservation Act of 1966 it became eligible for protection under Section 106 of that Act. Within this district, the Old Ursuline Convent and Jackson Square have been singled out as individual structures of national significance. These are but two of other historical and architectural potentially nationally significant structures within this district such as the old United States Mint, conveyed by the United States Museum about two years ago.

Evaluation of the problem
Rader and Associates, Engineers and Architects of New Orleans and Miami, Florida, proposed five alternative schemes at the request of the

Louisiana Department of Highways on the construction of Inter-State 310 along the east side of the Vieux Carré. These include: elevated; surface; rolling; and depressed. All of these schemes except the depressed scheme, however, call for roadbeds which rise to a height of forty-five feet south of Governor Nicholls Street, or roughly twenty feet above the French Market buildings.

Opinion of the National Register
'Basically, the road should not be constructed along the proposed route at all.
1. One of the needs this road is supposed to fill is to take heavy traffic out of the historic district. The bulk of the traffic in the Vieux Carré, except during brief rush hours, is made up of visitors and local residents, none of whom have great need for a new highway.
2. If the highway is above ground it will restrict future developments and if those developments remove the commercial enterprises in the area there will be even less advantage to these schemes.
3. Much has been said about the relative costs involved in these schemes. From a preservation standpoint the cost of the road cannot be measured against the loss in aesthetic and historical values caused by the construction. If the engineer's main concern is cost, there is a sixth alternative — building no road.
4. By using Inter-State 10 and the Pontchartrain Expressway, motorists can now bypass the Vieux Carré if they desire to do so. This proposed highway, because of the turns that have to be made to skirt the Vieux Carré and the river, would appear to save only about two-thirds of a mile, provided the motorist is going from the intersection of Inter-State 10 and Elysian Fields to the Greater New Orleans Bridge. Otherwise, it will be the long way around.'

The above statement was made when the Department of Transportation in Washington was constrained to take into account the effect of the proposed expressway on National Register Property, in this case the old French Quarter of the town. It should be noted that the Federal Government would bear most of the cost of construction.

The history of the proposed facility is long and complicated. With the opposition to it growing, the idea of an elevated expressway was abandoned by the protagonists in favour of a 'ground-level scheme' (ground-level in front of Jackson Square and for some distance on either side) which raised questions as to whether it would actually be seen and heard from the French Quarter. The City Council voted four to three in its favour.

Owing to continued local and national opposition, a final alternative was then considered which consisted essentially of depressing the roadbed for a considerable distance. The Port Authority had objections to the depressed scheme.

'There is no doubt that the depressed scheme would be most harmful to port operation both during the long construction period and for all time thereafter. The period during construction would deprive the Port Commission of a large amount of revenues from the affected wharves, their principal source of income. During construction there would be other greater and far reaching effects — the loss in man-hours of work that effects the entire economy of the area, the temporary abandonment of the wharves for the time requiring relocation of the shipping agencies having use of them which might be the cause of an expensive rehabilitation programme — these and whatever other effects that would be created, add to a tremendous sum that is a debit to the economy of New Orleans and the area. The depressed scheme is not compatible with the continuing need to maintain the Bienville Street and Governor Nicholls Street Wharves in service and would require the abandonment of such wharves. For these reasons, the Port Commission has indicated that the depressed scheme would not be acceptable to it.'

In the spring of 1969, the Advisory Council on Historic Preservation was called, as required under Section 106 of the Historic Preservation Act. After a lengthy public meeting in Washington and three days spent on the site, the Council made its recommendation, which was essentially adverse, although the depressed scheme was considered to be the only acceptable solution if a highway was finally to be built.

It is believed that the comment of the Advisory Council was instrumental in the Secretary of Transportation's decision. The *New York Times* of 10th July 1968 summed it up this way:

'VOLPE VETOES A FREEWAY TO SAVE FRENCH QUARTER IN NEW ORLEANS: Secretary of Transportation John A. Volpe has refused to grant Federal funds for part of the Inter-State Highway System that would have "seriously impaired the historic quality of New Orlean's famed French Quarter". He also held that an alternative depressed route was not acceptable because of what he called its disruptive effects on the city, excessive costs and construction hazards to the Mississippi River levée the protects the entire city. His ruling was believed to be the first denial of federal funds for a highway on the basis of preserving an historic area.

The significance, however, was said to go far beyond historic preservation.

Opposition to the New Orleans freeway plan is representative of what urban and highway planners consider revolution among city dwellers, particularly Negroes and the poor, against the destruction of inner city neighbourhoods. Other examples are plans for expressways in a dozen or more cities, including Cambridge, Massachusetts near Harvard University, San Francisco, Washington and Baltimore. Some officials speculated that Secretary Volpe would be reviewing more plans that affect inner city neighbourhoods. The controversy over the New Orleans plans was sparked by national groups interested in preserving historic sites and by national conservation groups opposed to urban highways that impair the quality of the environment and add to pollution problems. By his ruling, Mr Volpe overturned the Department's Federal Highway Administration, which had recommended the depressed roadway in the last days of the Johnson Administration.

Mr Volpe issued a statement saying that "a careful review of the highway proposed and the position of various interests concerned convinced me that the public benefits from the highway would not be enough to warrant damaging the treasured French Quarter".

The cost of the proposed 3.4-mile elevated section through the Vieux Carré, or French Quarter, and the Jackson Park Square area as an extension of Inter-State Highway 310 has been set at about $31 million. The depressed roadway would cost $12.4 million more.

The President's Advisory Council on Historic Preservation had recommended either a new route for Inter-State 310 or the depressed roadway as an alternative. Council members include Mr Volpe and six other Cabinet officers.'

Conclusion
A national council on historic preservation which includes as its members heads of federal departments of transportation, public works and commerce, as well as of federal cultural institutions on education, the arts and the humanities, can thus be influential in decision-making processes involving highway planning, especially when the departments concerned are constrained to take into account the effect upon cultural property listed in the national protective inventory of all federal, federally-assisted or licensed undertaking.

Incorporated Trusts and Societies

Although the requirements of the new laws brought the Department of Transportation and federal intervention into the Vieux Carré case, and the historic quarter was spared the intrusion of a highway, one can assume that little would have been accomplished without the activities of local societies and individuals to whom the French Quarter was not only a tremendous tourist attraction but also a cherished part of their city's historic and architectural heritage. As the Fordham Law Review put it in 1961, 'A desire exists to preserve the beauty of these districts quite apart from the incidental economic benefits resulting thereby. It is time that the courts recognised that the very preservation of historical monuments, the beauty of the settings in which they are placed and the beauty of our communities as a whole is an end in itself'.

Until quite recently it was assumed by the public that a local historical society would be the agent for local preservation. As Sumner Appleton forecast, this has not always proved to be the case. Traditionally, the chief interest of these societies has been in genealogy and museum collections. New organisations have had to be formed for active preservation, such as the Providence Preservation Society, the Historic Charleston Foundation, or the Old Heritage Foundation of Deerfield, Massachusetts. A typical organisation is that of Old Salem, Inc. founded in 1950 to restore the Moravian community already mentioned. It has been active in rerouting traffic off the main street of the village, placing electric wires underground, and numerous other enterprises in addition to restoration. No federal help has been sought, but some $6 million has been spent in bringing back a decaying community to life. Old Salem receives over 100,000 visitors a year.

These private trusts and foundations are usually incorporated under State law, and to be tax-free must engage only in charitable and educational work. In most States they may own, lease or sell properties, which may be the most important part of their operations. Finding new uses for restored or rescued buildings is also a prime occupation of these groups.

In the case of the Providence Preservation Society, federal help was sought to demonstrate how rehabilitation and renewal could be accomplished in historic areas, specifically in College Hill, an older residential district incorporating the first settlement of the town. This influential study, which preceded the new historic preservation legislation by ten years, was paid for partly by popular subscription and partly by the Urban Renewal Administration. Private enterprise restored over seventy-five houses in the area at a cost of nearly $1.5 million. One of the objectives of the College Hill study was to show how contemporary architecture could fit into a historical background. This was done by drawings, and later some demonstrations were made by architects sympathetic to the idea. Unfortunately, new buildings in the historic district did not always pay heed to the injunction to be

98

good neighbours:

> 'In preparation for the building of its Rockefeller Library, Brown
> University (a private institution) came before the Historic District
> Commission to ask permission to demolish an early federal house on
> the second priority list of the zoning ordinance. The Commission
> reluctantly granted this permission since the full set of completed
> plans for the library was based on the removal of the building. The
> library loading platform now replaces this house and unfortunately
> faces a historic residential group across the street.'
> (*College Hill.* A Demonstration Study of Historic Area Renewal. City
> Plan Commission, Providence, 2nd ed. 1967, p.228.)

Because of the attractiveness of College Hill as an old quarter of fine
houses close to the downtown business district, the rehabilitated
houses have easily found new owners who keep them in residential
use, although there is also some institutional use (there are no less than
four colleges in the immediate vicinity).

Historic District Legislation

Historic district legislation in the United States allows a place for
the *genius loci*. Not every part need be historically or architecturally
significant. 'Historic district architectural controls', according to the
New England lawyer and preservationist Albert B. Wolfe, 'aim at
preserving appearance without change in ownership or use; where the
setting is important as well as the buildings, or the relationship to each
other of a sufficient number of historic buildings creates a whole that
is greater than the sum of its parts'.

Beginning with the already-mentioned Historic District of Charleston,
South Carolina, in 1931, the idea progressed slowly until after
World War II, when it gained momentum with the interest of northern
cities in the legal device (*vide* Providence, previously cited). By 1969,
according to the records of the National Trust in Washington, forty-five
out of fifty States had enabling legislation. Some States, *e.g.* Texas,
do not need enabling legislation to designate historic districts. The total
of all districts, within counties, within cities or city-wide, created by
municipal ordinance at the time of writing, is estimated to be over 200.

The United States courts have tended to uphold regulations applying
to historic districts, particularly if they are well-drawn. The
Massachusetts Supreme Court in two advisory opinions held that the
State legislatures had the power to establish these districts and to
impose architectural controls.

The judicial opinion noted their tourist (and therefore economic)

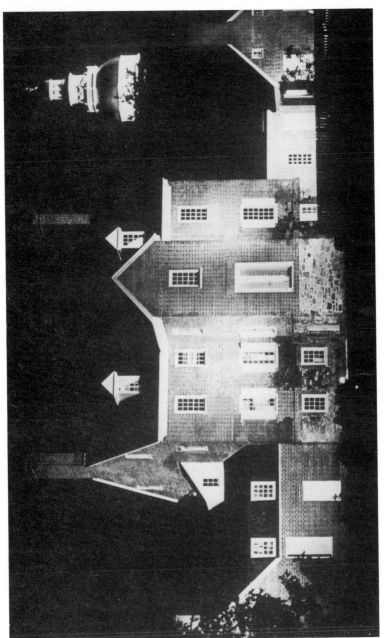

William Paca mansion, Annapolis, Maryland

value and quoted the 'right to be beautiful' opinion of the Supreme Court of the United States. In the matter of the Massachusetts legislation, the judges concluded that the law contained sufficient standards and noted the historical significance of the Beacon Hill district of Boston. This was one of the first two districts to be established, and proved so successful that it was enlarged twice. In the opinion of Professor Norman Williams of Rutgers University it is in the historic districts that a solid legal basis for architectural control will appear in the United States, a country hitherto known for its suspicion of a public aesthetics superimposed on private property.[4]

The controls vary somewhat from State to State, but Massachusetts can serve as an example. After a committee has surveyed and documented an area, the local government appoints a commission, which is similar to an architectural board of review. The commission is directed to consider *inter alia* 'the general design, arrangement, texture, materials, colour' of the district's buildings, 'but not detailed designs, relative size of buildings, interior arrangement or building features not subject to the public view'. Each district is to have specific boundaries. Any proposed new construction or alteration visible from a public street has to be approved by the commission, which also has control over demolition and advertising signs.

One of the most interesting historic districts in Massachusetts is the Back Bay in Boston, an elegant urban residential creation of the second half of the nineteenth century on filled land. When the neighbourhood association first applied for Historic District designation on the basis of the area's literary and other historical associations, it was turned down by the city council. Applying again, but this time on the basis of architectural importance, the designation was granted. It is noteworthy that in this, as in most other cases, the impetus came from a group of residents concerned about the future of their neighbourhood, which in the example of the Back Bay, was becoming a district of boarding houses and college dormitories with a transient population.

Rehabilitation: Commercial Uses

The rehabilitation of commercial districts has proved to be the most difficult of all historical revitalisation problems. Local governments and merchants' associations have preferred a clean sweep to the delicate surgery needed to upgrade a nineteenth-century business block which has the charm of old brick buildings with their elaborate cornices and quaint shop-fronts. This is partly an economic question. In the United States, these older blocks are prime targets for new car parks and garages, since their location is usually in or near the central business district of today.

A recent conference on relocation which dealt with small businesses noted that many enterprises that were liquidated during the building of new urban freeways might have continued if they had not been displaced.[5] The city district presents more problems than the museum village, where small shops catering to the tourist trade can be most successful.

However, there are many examples of successful commercial renewal retaining historic buildings in the big cities, Ghiradelli Square in San Francisco being an excellent case. The present owners of an old chocolate factory, which was a favourite local landmark, became concerned that much of San Francisco was being destroyed. They used the old building and several related ones to form a complex of shops and restaurants around a central plaza, served by an underground parking garage for 300 cars. A new structure was added, modern in appearance but in keeping with the red brick of the old factory buildings. The Square has become a prime tourist attraction, by night as well as by day. San Franciscans are somewhat divided over the appropriateness of the large electric sign, but this has been a fixture of the local scene for half a century and many people do not want to see it go. During the day, the fountains, flowers and trees help to make the new square a place for leisurely strolling in the California sunshine.

A more ambitious restoration is taking place in Boston. The historic Faneuil Hall-Quincy Market complex, designed by the architect Alexander Parris in 1824 and one of the most distinguished examples of the Greek Revival style in the United States, will form the centre of a six-acre historic district which will include small shops and offices, outdoor cafes, restaurants and a pedestrian mall. The Federal Government has provided a $2.1 million dollar grant for this project to the Boston Redevelopment Authority for the exterior renovation, while private investment of $10 to $12 million will be sought for the interior remodelling. The office rentals are to be competitive with those in new construction.

In smaller cities, commercial rehabilitation has functioned best when the merchants have reached a mutual agreement to fix up their shop-fronts, adopt a uniform size and location of signs and have local ordinances enacted to control the exterior appearance of the street or block.

Rehabilitation: Housing

The conversion and rehabilitation of old houses either for single family occupancy or into apartments has received more attention since housing policy began to change in the late 1950s in response to public outcries against wholesale demolition. Various experts have

Society Hill, Philadelphia: restored houses

provided evidence of a continuing need for old housing, and others have advocated maintenance and remodelling of old structures rather than clearance and redevelopment.[6] Some have gone so far as to say that the most promising stimulation of demand for housing in the central city is the symbolic value of its historic buildings and monuments.[7] Social scientists have helped to save old neighbourhoods indirectly by publishing studies of former occupants who have been uprooted in the course of clearance and redevelopment. These people have often revealed a loss of identity by being removed from their former living quarters, social clubs and contacts. One survey showed that the former neighbourhood provided continuity and was central to the residents' conception of themselves and of the world outside.[8]

Concern over social loss has caused some government officials to turn to historic preservation of some sites òf special significance to minority groups', reports an assistant secretary of the Department of Housing and Urban Development. This official goes on to say:

'We can complement current efforts to "rediscover" the forgotten contributions that such groups have made to the history of this country . . . By combining architectural variety and historical significance, restored buildings can rejuvenate a city. In addition, historic preservation often stimulates private restoration and tourist interest while conserving the best features of the man-made environment.'[9]

One of the early renewal efforts of this kind, now completed, was the Wooster Square district of New Haven, Connecticut, in which the population was largely of Italian origin, albeit by this time second and third generation as well. The district, however, was much older than the first wave of Italian immigration to the city. Most of the properties were owned by people who would have liked to improve them, but until federal urban renewal made financing possible, the banks would not lend money to the home-owners in what was considered in financial circles to be a run-down, decaying district. When in 1954 the Housing Act was amended to permit rehabilitation as a method of renewal, planning funds were made available for this district and, over a period of several years, a comprehensive programme of commercial, industrial, residential and educational rehabilitation and development took place. Sketches of how the buildings should look were prepared by a resident architect in a field office. Housing codes were enforced under this urban renewal programme and provided a firm basis for interior rehabilitation, but rehabilitation of the exteriors was entirely voluntary. Some new housing was built, but in small pockets. Commercial establishments were mostly allowed to remain, and a new industrial district was created in a blighted area of mixed uses, which was cleared by the Redevelopment Agency's powers of eminent domain.

Around the relatively intact early nineteenth-century square there was a group of fine houses — one, for instance, by the architect Henry Austen (1804-91) being of Tuscan block design with Indian Islamic details. Austen's drawings are in the Yale University library, so that it was comparatively easy to make an authentic exterior restoration, including a return to the original paint colour. The interior has been converted into apartments.

Although the residents of today have no connection with the early builders and owners, there is a strong local feeling in the Wooster Square district. Does the architecture play a part in encouraging this sense of identification? Although it was not originally a part of their cultural heritage but of the vanished Anglo-American merchants who built the square, they have come to consider it so. They have absorbed the architectural character as a symbol of their life-style.

In the State of Connecticut where this development lies, it is necessary to obtain the consent of 75 per cent of the property owners before a historic district can be designated, with all the restrictions on property which this entails. (See above for a description of the Massachusetts law). When the privately-supported New Haven Preservation Trust recently spear-headed a movement to designate a historic district around Wooster Square, thus reinforcing urban renewal, approval of over 90 per cent of the owners was obtained. This says something for the educational work of the Trust in convincing the doubtful that they had something important to preserve, but it says more for the owners' good sense in taking the necessary action to enhance both their cultural patrimony and the public welfare.

San Antonio, Texas

San Antonio is a city of contrasts. La Villita, a two-hundred-year-old restored Spanish village, stands in the shadows of the city's tallest skyscrapers. The river walk along the San Antonio river has small curio shops, sidewalk cafes, grassy tree-lined banks and Spanish plazas; on the street level, 9 metres above, a metropolitan area of 700,000 people carries on its normal hurried life. Over half the population is of Latin descent and many are of Chinese and German origin.

A World Fair was held in San Antonio in 1968. The designers decided to make full use of historic structures in preparing the site. A large number of them, representing a variety of cultural and architectural influences, were grouped in an area which it was decided to use as the Fair's international section. The City of San Antonio assumed the costs of restoration; the buildings were adapted for use by exhibitors and others, but without any loss of authenticity or individuality. To a certain extent they influenced the design of other buildings on the Fair site. There could be no question of competing with the colonnaded facades and other architectural trappings of the existing buildings. Consequently the design of the dominant structures of the Fair (the Convention and Community Center, the Tower of the Americas, and the Texas and United States Pavilions) were simple. Each was a handsome structure which complemented the buildings around it and so helped to illustrate the theme of the Fair: the Confluence of the Civilisations in the Americas.

The old buildings evoke the nostalgic charm of early San Antonio. During the Fair they served as foreign restaurants, tea houses, boutiques and exhibit areas. Today they continue to function in various roles while providing a permanent reminder of San Antonio's colourful history.

The Convention and Community Center; the 210-metre high Tower of the Americas with its revolving restaurant and observation decks, the Museum of Texan Cultures, and the United States Pavilion (which may become a federal courts building) compose, with the old buildings that have been preserved, one of the most significant concentrations of civic structures in America.

NOTES

1. Richard C. Wade: *The Urban Frontier*, 1959, p.206.
2. *See* Almont Lindsay: *The Pullman Strike*, Chicago, 1942; and Wayne Andrews: *The Battle for Chicago*, New York, 1946.
3. Charles B. Hosmer: *Presence of the Past*, New York, 1966.
4. Norman Williams, Jr.: *The Structure of Urban Zoning*, New York, 1966.
5. *Relocation: Social and Economic Aspects*, Special Report 110, Highway Research Board, Washington DC, 1970.
6. Bernard J. Frieden: *The Future of Old Neighborhoods*, Cambridge, Mass., 1964.
7. Walter Firey: *Land Use in Central Boston*, Cambridge, Mass., 1947, pp.324/5.
8. Marc Fried: 'Grieving for a Lost Home' in *The Urban Condition*, ed. L.J. Duhl, New York, 1963.
9. *HUD Challenge,* Washington DC, Nov-Dec/1970, p.5.

Further Reading:
Charles Abrams: *The City is the Frontier,* New York, 1965.
City Plan Commission: *College Hill,* Providence, R.I., 2nd. ed., 1967.
Robert J. Garvey and Terry B. Morton: 'The United States Government in Historic Preservation', in *Monumentum,* Vol.2, 1968, Louvain, Belgium.
Stephen W. Jacobs: 'Governmental Experience in the United States', in *Historic Preservation Today,* Charlottesville, Va., 1966.
Walter M. Whitehill: 'The Right of Cities to be Beautiful', in *With Heritage So Rich,* A Report of a Special Committee on Historic Preservation under the Auspices of the United States Conference of Mayors, Washington DC, 1966.

6.   JAPAN: TWO ANCIENT CAPITALS AND THE MENACE TO THEM

Teiji Itoh and Koji Nishikawa

The cultural heritage of most Japanese cities is menaced today by economic and social pressures.

The traditional Japanese home is built of unpainted wood and is usually one, rarely two, stories high. Wooden screens with paper panels *(shoji)* make partitions inside. In fine weather, the light construction, and surrounding gardens and walks made a very attractive combination. But it is difficult to install central heating, and houses which use traditional methods of heating tend to be uncomfortable in winter. People normally sit on mats on the floor; quilts are used for sleeping and rooms are generally free of furniture. This pattern is changing, however. Younger people in Japan are on the average taller than before. The scale of the traditional building is less suitable and they prefer to use western-style chairs, tables and other furniture. Many other changes have been taking place in Japan during the past fifty years, and change has accelerated rapidly in the past ten to twenty years. Economic and demographic changes in particular have greatly affected both town and countryside.

Origins of Domestic Architecture

The use of iron was introduced into the islands of Japan at about 200 BC, at the same time as wet-rice agriculture. The first established settlements consisted of pit houses, semi-subterranean structures characteristic of the earlier Neolithic period. They were the earliest type of domestic architecture. The iron tools and mortise-and-tenon joints allowed more elaborate building. Agriculture gradually displaced hunting and gathering as the main source of food, and various types of shrine and palace architecture evolved. The cultural centre of Japan moved from the northern part of the island of Kyushu to the Kinki area (the present Nara − Kyoto − Osaka area) of Honshu, the principal island of Japan.

The Kofun or tumulus period lasted roughly from the fourth century to the beginning of the seventh. Various groups unified under a single ruler, and a dynasty became the Imperial Family. The tumuli were monumental burial mounds for members of the upper class; there are some 4,600 of them in the Prefecture of Nara.

Centralisation was almost complete when Buddhist architecture was introduced in the sixth century from the mainland. One of the palaces built at the time, the Asuka-Itabuku-Gu, is now being excavated. Large wooden buildings began to be built, and these provided the origin for future developments in Japanese architecture. An outstanding wooden structure of the period is the Horyu-ji temple (seventh century), the oldest extant example of Japanese architecture. It reflects styles that were current in China during the sixth century.

Nara and Kyoto, Ancient Capital Cities

Nara was the capital during the Heijo period (710-84 A.D.). It was 4.3 km wide (east to west) and 4.8 km long (north to south). The houses of nobles and aristocrats were centred about the palace. Large markets were located in the eastern and western districts. At its peak, the city had a population of about 200,000 people, including thousands of servants and guards, and many of the most important surviving temples were built (Yakushiji, Toshodaiji, Hokkeji, Gangoji and Kofukuji). Its period of greatness continued under the reign of seven emperors, until the capital was transferred to Nagaoka. Even then, Nara remained important, because of the Kofukuji and Kasuga, the tutelary temple and shrine of the powerful Fujiwara family. Although much of the city was razed by fire at the end of the twelfth century, the power and wealth of the temples enabled it to survive the holocaust, and it remained one of the most important cultural centres during the early mediaeval period.

In the middle of the late medieval period (seventeenth century), guidebooks for tourists were published and widely read. Nara was not only a sacred city but a centre for sight-seeing. In the nineteenth century, the campaign against Buddhist images during the Meiji restoration damaged many of the temples. The Kofukuji temple in particular suffered badly. Except in the central quarter, buildings were converted into government offices. About 1880, an interest in conservation developed, and government grants were provided for the preservation of ancient temples and shrines, and the restoration of Kofukuji was planned. The repair of the Hall of the Great Buddha (Todai-ji) was sponsored by private funds. Nara Park was planned. In 1895 the Imperial Museum of Nara was founded and, in the next year, the Ancient Temples and Shrines Preservation Act was adopted.

The historical development of Kyoto was as follows. In 652, Naniwa-kyo, the first capital city in Japan, was built, followed by others: Fujiwara-kyo (694), Heijo-kyo (710), Nagaoka-kyo (784) and Heian-kyo (794). Kyoto was established as the capital at the end of the eight century, and took the T'ang capital of Chungsang as a model. The Imperial Palace was the nucleus, and an avenue running south of the Palace provided the central axis. The Chinese grid pattern of the streets was not adhered to; where streets were not required, dwellings or farms remained. Many villas and temples were built outside the city proper. With Buddhism, the continental style of architecture with stone foundations and tiled roofs reached Japan. The grid pattern was also used in the surrounding rice fields. Large wooden buildings provided a pattern for future architecture. An outstanding example of monumental wooden temple architecture is the Todai-ji Temple in Nara; it includes the largest wooden structure in the world (the Hall of the Great Buddha) and a pagoda 100 metres high.

Various styles developed. Governmental architecture was based on the Buddhist temple. Shinden (residential hall) architecture provided the new mode for aristocratic residences. The five-storey pagoda at Daigo-ji Temple and the Hoo-do Temple (Phoenix Hall) of Byodo-in Temple were built. The Jeian-jingu Shrine (1895) is an imitation, on a smaller scale, of the Daigoku-den (eight century) built in the Heian capital. But traditional Shinto building also continued.

The feudal era began with the founding of the Kamakura Bakufu by Minamotono-Yoritomo in 1185, and two new styles (Tenjiku and Karayo), from the Sung Dynasty in China, were introduced into Japan. The Minami-Daimon (south gate) of the Todai-ji in Nara is Tenjiku; the Garan (Buddhist Hall) of the Tofuku-ji Temple in Kyoto is Karayo.

Old and new co-existed, influencing and changing each other, giving rise to new derivative styles. The history of Japanese architecture shows a continuous blending of heterogeneous cultural elements which frequently yielded a very harmonious result.

At the end of the sixteenth century, feudalism entered a new phase. Castles, mausoleums, and Shoin-style houses, were built more than temples and the original forms of present-day town houses appeared. Kyoto underwent many changes during the medieval period, during which there were bloody conflicts, and various shifts of population. After the Shogunate was transferred to Edo (modern Tokyo) in the seventeenth century, Kyoto's prosperity depended on the Nishijin textile industry. In the early eighteenth century, it lost its dominant position as Osaka became the commercial centre of Japan. Despite all this, Nara and Kyoto still remained the cultural centres of Japan throughout the nineteenth century.

Under the Meiji restoration (1868), when the Emperor officially became head of the State, Tokyo finally replaced Kyoto as the capital. Wooden architecture predominated during the nineteenth and early twentieth centuries in Nara and Kyoto. The Japanese had been interested in brick and stone buildings from the eighteenth century, and a vain attempt to popularise them was made for a short time around the middle of the nineteenth. But brick and stone proved impractical because of frequent earthquakes, and high summer temperatures and humidity. On the other hand, the light wooden domestic houses have rarely survived or been preserved.

The mid-nineteenth century produced a completely different influence: western architecture. This influence can be seen in Kyoto and Nara in some schools, residences, stores, inns, churches, museums, factories, post offices, banks, prisons. However, the total was relatively small. Buildings of the Meiji era (1868–1912) still standing number only fifty-two in Kyoto and ten in Nara; and domestic architecture was not greatly affected. In fact, traditional wooden houses and farms continued to be built until about 1945, and contributed greatly to the beauty and skylines of both cities.

Fundamental changes have been taking place since. Buildings with reinforced concrete steel frames and curtain walls that are fire- and earthquake-resistant began to replace wooden structures at an accelerated pace after 1950. Before, homes and shops were mostly two-storied; legal and structural regulations made it difficult and expensive to build wooden houses any higher. Growing needs (floor space to meet expanded commercial needs, car parks, highways) and rising land prices combined to make the survival of the wooden house impractical.

Kyoto and Nara were affected in many respects. There have been changes in the building materials used. Earth, wood and tiles have given way to concrete, steel, glass and plastic. The skyline has changed; the old symmetry of low-lying structures is broken. Traditional wooden buildings have steep, tiled roofs and sharply-projecting eaves; concrete and steel buildings are mostly box-shaped and lack dramatic projection.

Causes of Deterioration

Under urban conditions, the average life of a traditional Japanese house is forty years. Fire, earthquakes and other hazards shorten the average. People used to cherish Yamatoumune-style farmhouses, of which forerunners have been discovered in archaeological excavations; they fitted in harmoniously with the surrounding countryside. They are becoming increasingly rare today because of rising land costs and population pressures.

Architecturally scheduled and historically important monuments of Kyoto and Nara are protected by the Government. But with the loss of so many which are unscheduled, and the disappearance of traditional domestic architecture, the appearance and the character of the two cities are changing. Industrialisation and commerce may be much more developed in many other cities in Japan, but irreversible changes have taken place in Kyoto and Nara. Blocks of high-rise, reinforced concrete buildings have blotted out rivers and streams that once

110

An old temple and a new apartment house: Chionji and its surrounding area near Hyakumanben.

coursed through the towns, and turned them into underground sewers, leaving in their place a harsh and sterile urban reality.

Modern buildings, frequently void of aesthetic quality, show up badly near older, more graceful buildings in the historic quarters of the two cities. The skyline, with its hills, pagodas and temples, is shattered here and there by monolithic cubic masses of concrete and glass. The mountains can no longer be seen from the centre.'If this continues uncontrolled, the two historically and aesthetically renowned cities will soon be irretrievably spoiled.

The menace is twofold: externally, from urbanisation and industrialisation; internally, from causes that are intrinsic to historic cities. The growth of the population in the Kyoto-Osaka-Kobe area led to real estate development around Kyoto and Nara (which are within reach for commuters). The countryside is undergoing drastic changes. The industrialised coastal zone is penetrating inland, with effects that are more profound and far reaching than any since the nineteenth century.

These general problems are common to other historic cities in Japan. Nara and Kyoto, approximately 40 kilometres apart, also have specific problems which differ in detail because of the different historic traditions of the two cities, and their different economies and administrations.

Differences between Nara and Kyoto

The Nara Basin includes eight cities and one village. This complicates preservation, as it demands co-operation and joint planning by several autonomous units. But nearly all of the Kyoto Prefecture lies within the limits of the city itself.

In 1964, a man who had bought the historic Narabi hill area in Nara wanted either to build an engineering college or use it as a cemetery. Permission was refused. In 1969, the Telegraph and Telephone Corporation planned to erect a 90-metres high building only 400-metres from To-ji Temple, a famous and beautiful five-storied pagoda. The authorities insisted on moving the site to a distance of 2,000 metres.

In contrast to Nara, the greatest changes in Kyoto are explained by internal causes rather than pressures from Osaka. The numbers working in primary industries fell by 218,000 to the present 16,000 during the past twenty-five years, but rose in secondary industries from 75,000 to 276,000 and in tertiary industries from 102,000 to 358,000. There are few factories in Kyoto, and no immediate development plans. Existing factories do not spoil the sites, but air pollution (especially sulphurous acid gas from factories) has been affecting metal used in architecture, and art objects in shrines and temples.

Apart from the historically and artistically important religious structures and the buildings of the nobility and aristocracy, both basins had their villages and hamlets. Wet-rice agriculture provided the primary crop. The farming communities still exist. The dark grey-brown tiled roofs and unpainted weathered walls offer a pleasant and harmonious contrast to the changing colours of the rice fields. Farmers and their families working in the fields added the colour of their traditional costumes to the scene. Low-cost housing units have now substituted red tiles, or other garishly-coloured roofs. Buildings are cheap and ill-designed. Small ugly factories dot the countryside. The result is as aesthetically depressing to the visitor as it must, in the long run, likewise prove to residents.

It will be convenient at this point to consider Nara and Kyoto separately:

Nara

Around 1950, as a result of a rapid and remarkable process of urbanisation, the principal trends of change became clearly visible in the Nara Basin. Changes in land use led to the destruction of cultural properties, the disappearance of historic areas, and drastic alterations in the landscape; the reasons for the changes were real estate development, tourist growth, and new industry, public works and urbanisation.

Real estate development is the most dramatically destructive factor. As industry and population expand in Osaka, building estates begin to cover farm lands and hills in most of the Nara Basin (especially near the railways). In the process archaeological sites may be lost or ruined, and even if protected and preserved, monuments lose associations and appeal as neighbouring buildings are demolished. Piecemeal development has begun to spoil what has been orderly patterns in villages and towns.

About 1955, housing for commuters to Osaka was built by a private railway company in the hilly area west of Nara. This was soon followed by medium-height apartment houses, built by public authorities, and others by private contractors. The western hills lost their former appearance. Similar changes subsequently took place in the flat area around the old Heijo capital, destroying historic sites and monuments in Kashihara, Asuka and Ikaruga. Ancient tombs and old kiln sites disappeared. Not only was the characteristic landscape of the basin altered but also the architectural harmony between its rural and urban elements. Little consideration was given to styles, colours, textures or design relationships or their effects on the environment into which they intruded.

Catering for tourists has long been one of Nara's important industries. There was a sharp growth after the railway between Osaka and Nara was built at the end of the nineteenth century and, during the past few years, the number of visitors has increased on an average of 8 per cent a year (an estimated total of 20 million in 1969). The majority concentrate on Nara itself and its vicinity, but increasing numbers now also visit the Asuka and Ikaruga districts. Most spend just a day, returning to hotels in Osaka and Kyoto the same night. This is too short to be of much commercial benefit locally. Travel organisations have been trying to get people to stay longer. In 1956, a group of hotels was built on the top of Mount Wakakusa. They unfortunately spoiled one of the most scenic areas of the basin, which included the urban area, Nara Park and two mountains — Wakakusa and Kasuga — which were associated with Nara in classical, historical and literary themes.

Again, an amusement park built in 1961 and a bowling alley clash strongly in style with the historical city. Older hotels were garishly remodelled to attract attention and clients. Other unfortunate results have followed ill-considered tourist development. Automobiles and large buses are a menace. Car parks take up a great deal of space; underground garages may have to be built at the more popular sites. Nara has had to limit the number of the cars which can enter. Some better system of sightseeing transport must be devised.

In 1949 the city of Nara built the Wakakusa Junior High School on the site of Tamon Castle, which has an important place in the history of Japan. Not only were the remains of the castle damaged but also the area around the tumulus of Emperor Shomu, located at the foot of the ruins. In 1961 plans were made for a private railway train depot on the site of Heijo Palace. Fortunately, this was strongly opposed by laymen and scholars, and the government eventually purchased the site. Two further projects — by-passes through the sites of the former Fujiwara Palace and the former Heijo Palace — were opposed. The decision on the first was suspended. The second was changed, the by-pass being re-routed to avoid the site. However, even a simple re-routing affected the ancient grid plan, which is unique in the country.

Since 1965, the Prefectural Office, the law court, and hotels, terminals and schools have been remodelled and converted into high-rise structures that affect the panorama. This could have been avoided by legislation and proper planning.

Local autonomy causes many preservation problems. Most local administrations obtain two-thirds of their income from the government, and one-third from local taxes. Improving their finances has usually meant increasing the possibility of obtaining money through rates and taxes from real estate, business and industry.

Before 1960 there were only a few textile and lumber mills in the Nara Basin. Several factories have since been built, following the

Government's decision to encourage the decentralisation of factories to areas which were relatively underdeveloped industrially. A new highway was opened, linking the industrial centres of Osaka and Nagoya. In 1964, an industrial district was established in Koriyama, followed by another in Nara itself, which now has factories manufacturing electric home appliances, machines and foods.

As each town or village wanted its industry, factories were built haphazard throughout the basin. Local authorities were invariably more interested in new industry than in plans to preserve cultural properties, historic sites and the natural environment. Recently, however, there has been some evidence of a reversal of this policy.

Nara is at a crucial period. Before it is too late, its heritage must be preserved, and some of its traditions revived and fostered. Archaeological surveys, methodically carried out since 1955, have revealed the structures and the dimensions of the Heijo Palace site. It is now classified and there are proposals to make it into an archaeological park. But building goes on, before the whole area has been thoroughly investigated. Further systematic investigations are urgently needed, so that a coherent policy for the Heijo Capitol can be devised and implemented. If nothing is done, the Nara Basin will become a dormitory for metropolitan Osaka, and be ruined by arbitrary industrial development. Its growth, unfortunately, is still largely haphazard.

Kyoto

Problems are similar in the Kyoto and Nara Basins. The grid pattern and traditional street names of the Heian Capitol still remain, but most of the archaeological sites and monuments are lost.

When Kyoto ceased to be the political and administrative centre of Japan, it still remained a major centre for the manufacture of textiles and for artisanal products. Following the Meiji Restoration (1868), however, and growing industrialisation, it lost the status it had enjoyed for over a thousand years. The city has since tried to find a new role. It has always had its tourists. In addition to institutions working on industrial problems (the Chemistry Institute and the Textile House, for example) it has many cultural and educational institutions: schools, universities, libraries, museums.

Attempts to introduce new industries did not meet with much success. Industry tended, instead, to concentrate in the coastal areas around Osaka and Kobe. This lack of success helped to preserve historic Kyoto. Urban development concentrated in suburban areas (the ancient Nagaoka capitol, the medieval religious town of Yamashin, the castle town of Fushim). Lack of controls nevertheless allowed many changes within the city, particularly in the

Street scenes in Kyoto

commercial centre.

The population of Kyoto, 1,100,000 in 1945, had reached 1,430,000 by 1970 and the urban area extended from 7,400 hectares to 8,230. Since 1960, private firms have been building low-cost housing in the western and eastern suburbs which tends to spoil the approaches to historic sites.

There is no large-scale urban development in Kyoto itself, but various areas have small-scale rebuilding schemes.

New buildings are limited in height to 20 metres in commercial districts. Historic monuments may be between 14 and 40 metres high and are often situated on high ground. If new buildings respect the height restrictions, and are kept separate, the ill-effects can be limited.

But the entrepreneurs are seldom worried about preserving the landscape or the traditional appearance of a city. And the architects do not ensure that new structures respect the general height level. The 1950 Building Standards Law limits the height of a penthouse to 12 metres, but neon signs and advertisements are frequently put up on top of them. Apartment houses and hotels are built on or near historic sites, not only because the neighbourhood is quiet but, quite frankly, to cash in on its reputation.

Development in Kyoto in the 1960s affected only a part of the city, but, in view of the proposed subway, is likely to be much more radical in the succeeding decade. Unless precautions are taken — methodical surveys and careful planning — large-scale works will ruthlessly destroy remains and the historical character of the city.

Kyoto has been famous for centuries. In 1969, it received 18,100,000 visitors, a 2 per cent increase over the previous year. As in Nara, the increase reflects increased leisure and higher standards of living in Japan; it also involves the usual dangers and, not least, from the ill-considered attractions that are provided.

In 1960, a kind of observatory, 848 metres high, with an ugly exterior, was erected on the summit of Mount Hiei, site of the famous Enryaku-ji Temple and one of the most exquisite spots in the Kyoto area. The finishing touch was added by transforming the surroundings into a recreational area of dubious taste. In 1969, despite an acrimonious campaign against it by Kyoto's defenders, a 131-metre high sight-seeing tower was built on top of a hotel in front of Kyoto station. Nishiyama Highway was built in 1965. Wooden hotels, with two or three storeys, were rebuilt higher in reinforced concrete, with disastrous aesthetic effects.

More cars in Kyoto mean fewer trams. Certain lines have been abolished, and a subway is under consideration. National Route 1 passes through Kyoto and by 1962 had reached saturation point. The Ministry of Construction plan for a new by-pass was opposed by many on the grounds that it would cross a section of the Otani mausoleum of Nishi-Hongan-ji Temple and screen the view of the historic sites on Higashiyama. But the opposition failed, and the by-pass was completed in 1967. To widen streets in order to take increased traffic, traditional town houses were pulled down on both sides of many streets, and new buildings replace them in different styles, texture and colour — sometimes disastrously, as in the area around Koryu-ji Temple.

By 1970, sixty-four pedestrian bridges had been put up. They have come in for much criticism. One in front of Sanjo Keihin Station in the central part of the city damages the perspective. Authorities in Kyoto and elsewhere in Japan seem to have given up the idea of allowing any more of them.

Drive-in restaurants have opened in the northern and northwestern suburbs, located some distance out because of parking difficulties in the more central areas. Some of these restaurants have flashy exteriors that are totally out of keeping with surrounding buildings.

Parking area plans at one time threatened the ancient system of canals. The police authorities wanted to provide a parking area in 1968 by covering up the Takase River, which runs through the centre of the city and has many associations; in 1954 there was a similar plan to cover up the Horikawa Canal. Fortunately, both plans were rejected by Kyoto's citizens. Parking has also affected temples and shrines — lots for cars and charter buses being provided, for example, within the precincts of some monuments. This is, of course, entirely undesirable, but such construction continues, *e.g.* at Tenryu-ji Temple in 1968. The Ministry of Culture, in 1969, warned Tenryu-ji that it must find another solution.

A proposed green belt around Kyoto. The Raku-nan green belt is based on three underlying ideas:

1. Kyoto should be made into a new cultural and educational centre for Japan by an expansion of the institutes for research, education and training upon which its development has depended since the mid-nineteenth century.
2. Facilities for enjoying Kyoto as a unique city should be improved by the work of institutes to be established for the evaluation, preservation and development of its cultural heritage.
3. Various national experimental laboratories and research institutes for the development of advanced industrial techniques should be set up in Kyoto.

The green belt is necessary to take in and link up many of the important monuments of Kyoto which are scattered round the slopes of the surrounding mountains. It would begin at the ruins of the

118

Nagaoka Palace and extend east to include the ruins of the Toba Villa and Fukakusa and then, running along the Nagoya-Kobe Highway, reach Daigo. It is essential to inhibit sprawling development on the periphery of the built-up area. Parking lots, inns or hotels and educational and cultural institutes would be provided at seven points in the green belt. These points, like the ancient 'Seven entrances to Kyoto' would serve as gates for traffic coming into the city. The northern part of the green belt would be zoned to preserve the best of the cultural heritage and historic landscape; the southern part would contain research institutes for both traditional and modern industries.

The green belt, with the Kyoto South intersection of the Nagoya-Kobe Highway as its centre, would link preservation and development. This central zone was the site of Toba Villa (whose structure is being revealed by the archeological excavations) which was once an outpost of Kyoto on the bank of the Yodo River in Toba. The present intersection was constructed tangentially to the site and ruins of Toba Villa, which would be preserved as a park, with a replica of the ancient city gate. A historical museum, a cultural centre and institutes could be built near the archaeological excavations) which was once an outpost groups) would not be limited to mere sightseeing. Finds from Toba Villa and the excavated floor pattern will, it is proposed, be placed on permanent display; and, in a corner of the museum garden, a house in the Shinden style of the late Heian period will be constructed.

The museum is to serve as a survey and research centre, and as the headquarters for the park administration and maintenance services. The cultural centre would be the administrative centre for all the museums in Kyoto. It would have two main departments: one for research and comparative cultural studies, the second for education (also open to visitors).

The museum park would contain two centres: one for traditional arts and crafts, situated near a college of arts with which it can co-operate; and one for traditional industries, *e.g.* Nishijin (textiles), Kiyomizu (porcelain), Fushimi (saké). Both would engage in research и and provide training. It is proposed that the arts and crafts centre should have working floor space that could be rented to various groups or institutions, and workshops that would be open to amateurs.

A science and technology research centre associated with Kyoto University will co-operate with the experimental industrial area in the south-west in pollution control experiments and the development of advanced industrial techniques — possibly for the entire country. A new city axis running through the experimental industrial area will provide a physical link with traditional industry.

A few kilometres to the west of this area is Nagaoka, which was the capital before Kyoto replaced it by imperial decree in 793. The

Yasaka Pagoda

former palace at Nagaoka is being excavated, but the survey should cover the whole area. If as seems likely, it reveals the characteristic grid pattern, this could provide the basic pattern for future planning in the area, which could incorporate all kinds of urban facilities – especially for children and the old – as well as accommodating high-rise residential buildings.

Entrances to Kyoto should be provided as in the former city, with a proper balance in the facilities respectively provided for cars and pedestrians. Monuments should not be preserved as isolated features but harmoniously incorporated in new, planned surroundings which reconcile the historical past of Kyoto with contemporary techniques and requirements.

The Need for an Official Policy

In September 1970, the Japanese National Commission for Unesco and the Agency of Cultural Affairs invited international and Japanese experts to a Symposium organised in co-operation with Unesco to discuss the whole question of historic quarters in the two cities. All the professions concerned were represented: architects, restorers, town planners, conservation experts, landscape architects, sociologists. The experts laid stress on two points in particular: the absence of a coherent preservation policy in current programmes in Japan; and the failure to take sufficient account of the interests and desires of people actually living in historic quarters.

Economic development had been highly successful in Japan, but a heavy price had been paid in terms of damage to the environment, and pollution. Kyoto and Mara had suffered, as neither legally nor administratively was the concept of a historic quarter recognised in Japan. Individual buildings or sites could be scheduled and protected, but not their surroundings.

A national land plan would provide the best framework for dealing on a large-scale and long-term basis with such problems as those raised by Kyoto and Mara. It would be possible, for example, to avoid the unplanned development which is fatally affecting both cities.

Unfortunately one effect of recent construction under national supervision has been too much standardisation and uniformity. This can be avoided by closer co-operation with local authorities.

The practical difficulties are many, however. The Cabinet tried to deal with co-ordination in 1957 and found that the particular interests of each Minister concerned were irreconcilable. The Minister of Culture had not the powers, the organisation or the specialists to deal effectively with the problems of urban development. One statistic is significant: in 1968 the land-use budget was 225 times the amount allotted for the preservation of cultural property. Under a coherent policy, money would have to be available from national, local and municipal sources (and possibly from foundations) to buy property which is threatened; to subsidise the maintenance or adaptation for other purposes of property in private hands; to finance the salvaging of buried cultural property endangered by public or private works; and to encourage the provision of facilities for tourists. The latter, obviously, can not only repay the investment but provide a handsome profit to the economy as a whole.

Five major Acts dealing with urban planning, preservation and tourist facilities have been passed since 1937, but they do not add up to a national policy. Similarly, architects and planners have produced seven major schemes for Nara and Kyoto alone since 1964. All, unfortunately tend to ignore the economic, social, ecological and psychological interests of people living in the historic quarters. One plan even went so far as to suggest that inhabitants should leave buildings, which would then remain empty as historic dwellings. The fact that buildings must keep their characteristic outside appearance does not mean that their inhabitants must also follow an outmoded way of life. As mentioned earlier, heating in winter is one problem. In general, however, not enough data has been collected about the traders and other residents in historic quarters. Until that is done, it is difficult to say what arts, crafts or other occupations should be introduced or encouraged. The Council of Europe's idea of a 'protective inventory' as referred to in Chapter 4 has proved very useful in Europe and could provide the basis for a rational programme.

The passage of cars through narrow streets is a problem in historic quarters of towns in all countries. Some have gone so far as to forbid it altogether. Where feasible, underground garages are an ideal solution.

Maintenance is a special difficulty in Japan because so many of the buildings to be preserved are wooden. Replacements have to be made by highly skilled carpenters. Fire is always a danger, and so are insects and fungi. It is interesting to note however that foreign experts at the Symposium considered that masonry in Europe often presents as many drawbacks as wooden structures in Japan. Stone from the same quarry can differ very considerably in quality, and may deteriorate under the effects of frost, damp, scaling and pollution.

A strong sense of family and community was always part of the traditional social structure in Japan. This is being increasingly affected by industrial growth. Younger people not only travel more than their parents did, but change their jobs and place of residence much more easily also. Japan has not escaped the social drawbacks of very rapid urbanisation. The preservation of historic quarters is, here as elsewhere, one of the ways of maintaining the sense of stability, continuity and identity of the inhabitants of cities which are growing too rapidly.

The preservation of historic quarters thus has physical, financial, aesthetic and social implications. Some aspects should be considered in a general national preservation policy. A great deal of expert knowledge is necessary and here the help of universities, learned bodies and various kinds of experts (including those working in industry) should be enlisted.

Industrialisation has many drawbacks which have been greatly emphasised in recent years – almost to the exclusion of the very real benefits it has brought to mankind. Luxuries once reserved for the few have become commonplace for the many. Much backbreaking work has been eliminated. Above all, the seven-day working week has disappeared for millions of people. Leisure is becoming a generally accepted right and, with leisure, ordinary people have become tourists. If they have cultural interests, they know what they want to see, and are accordingly natural supporters of preservation.

But the person who is a tourist for a small part of the year may defend quite different interests when at home. He may be less enthusiastic, for example, about supporting the preservation of a terrace of interesting houses if this goes against his own financial interests – even if his home town happens to be called Kyoto, Nara or Venice. In other words, much has to be done to educate the public. This kind of education is essentially long term, and the fact has to be faced that a certain percentage of people will always refuse such education. Morevoer, there is often no clear-cut line in the balance sheet: between the relative claims of what most people accept as progress and the much less clearly defined or evident reasons for preserving a site or building as an amenity that will serve the whole community. Kyoto and Nara are good examples of this continuing dilemma. Only in the wider perspective can it be clearly seen that the serious deterioration of either would be a loss not only to the city itself, or even Japan, but to the whole world.

The Breakthrough?

The seeds sown at the 1970 Symposium seem to have fallen on remarkably fertile ground. The detailed recommendations of the experts, and summaries of the papers and discussions were circulated. The Kyoto municipality, represented by observers at the discussions, invited the Council responsible for preserving the scenic beauty and historical sites of the city to review the various problems involved.

Following its recommendations, the municipality then adopted new regulations, in 1972. Several areas were zoned for protection and control, including those surrounding Gosho (the imperial palace),

Nijo Castle (former palace of the Tokugawa Shoguns) and some of the major temples. A stretch of Kamo river is to be protected, on the east bank, from the junction with its tributary, the Takonogawa north-east of the city, down to the railway bridge to the south-east, an area that includes the newly zoned historic quarter of Higashiyama-Sannenzaka. Other parts of the city will probably also be zoned.

The scheduling of historic quarters, by limiting building, commerce and industry in the areas affected, may result in a fall in the municipal revenue from rates and taxes, and also in losses to individual owners and enterprises. This may be offset by increased tourist revenue, direct and indirect.

Above all, the possibility of introducing national legislation to deal with problems similar to those of Nara and Kyoto all over the country is now under consideration. This could represent the real breakthrough, the guarantee that the inestimable artistic heritage of Japan will be rightly assessed in the national balance-sheet.

7.   TUNISIA: HOPES FOR THE MEDINA OF TUNIS

Jellal El Kafi

Except for such powers as they had under legislation for the protection of historic monuments, town planners, unable to intervene, have long had to look on helplessly as ancient towns changed, deteriorated, or were almost completely ruined. In an attempt to meet the town planner's problem, and take account of the whole urban fabric rather than the monument in isolation, the legislator came up with the new idea of renewal, combining cultural safeguarding with revitalisation.

Cultural desiderata conflict with socio-economic and everyday needs: expropriation and rehousing, to name only two, presuppose subsidy. A renewal scheme intended to take advantage of historic monuments and use the old urban shell for new purposes is not feasible without State subvention.

Rather than undertake a renewal scheme that would be seriously hampered by financial constraints, it seemed better, in the case of the Medina of Tunis to attempt rehabilitation, *i.e.* to adapt the organisation left by a vanished society for use in the conditions of present-day Tunisian society; for it must first be demonstrated, when growth and development priorities are being considered, that historical rehabilitation can contribute to economic expansion.

How can monuments inherited from the past be made to serve economic ends — since otherwise, their capacity to survive is doubtful? This is a primary question. A secondary one is of cultural values, of rehabilitation, since it is by no means self-evident that contemporary society will take over as its own the values of a community that broke up; rehabilitation implies a choice, the selecting of those values which remain vital. This precludes total conservation, and implies deliberate remodelling.

How can the old town be integrated with contemporary socio-economic, cultural and technological activities? It must be neither a ghetto nor the town's museum piece. In other words, environmental planning has to be reconciled with history.[1]

The approach in the case of the Medina of Tunis has been hesitant, and remains uncertain: proposed openings or demolitions that would allegedly create a better organised and healthier environment clashed with other plans to conserve facades and the general setting. The moderniser *versus* conservationist debate is basically sterile; town planners are now refusing the demolition-conservation dichotomy, and trying to work out more flexible and less arbitrary principles. This can best be done in the present case by examining the Medina of Tunis, past and present, from the point of view of several disciplines.

In 1928, the Cheran plan proposed a grid-iron layout for the Hafsia quarter, creating an open space in the Medina to admit motor traffic. In an article entitled 'La coordination des cités franco-musulmanes' published in *Tunisie 45*, A. Annabi wrote in 1945 that:

'if the blocks of Arab dwellings were less compact, and spaced out on much the same lines as in the European quarters, the inner rooms would have more fresh air from openings onto the street, and the patio would not have to be used in winter.... Houses should be grouped in such a way as to leave spaces wide enough for motor traffic, and permit proper underground drainage. Houses should be grouped around small green spaces or squares. The blocks should fit into a hexagonal plan, with streets arranged in a radial pattern, the blocks fitting together to produce a harmonious and well-ordered extension of the Arab town.'

An international competition in 1962 invited architects to submit schemes for driving a road through the Kasbah; fifty metres wide and passing at the foot of the Great Mosque, this was intended to link the European town with the administrative centre.

The rehabilitation project thus has economic, cultural and planning aspects, and the local authority and the State have to take responsibility for the future of the Medina and for dealing with the deterioration that has set in. The old town is being mutilated. The main threat is from the western-type organisation outside the Medina which has co-existed with it since the colonial period began, but has only made its full impact on the Medina since Tunisia became independent.

This article considers:
1. the traditional character of the Medina, and its cultural significance;
2. the relations between the historic Medina and the European town, and between it and the new town;
3. the rehabilitation problems that have to be dealt with by the local authorities and the State.

The Traditional Medina of Tunisia

Tunis is located on a narrow strip of land stretching between two lagoons, one to the east and one to the west, and closed to the north and south by hills. This strip of land lies on the major coastal route followed by migrations and pilgrimages between Barbary and Egypt. Carthage was too exposed seawards for the conquering Arabs; they preferred to settle on the site of the old Tounès (probably founded by the Berbers), situated at the inland end of the gulf and on the slopes of the hills overlooking the lagoons.

A particularly agreeable place of transit, Tunis was also a military strong point. Both open and enclosed, hospitable but easy to defend, it was here that the Jemaa Zitouna, the Mosque of the Olive Tree, was built, half way up a hill, where the east-west and north-south roads met; around the mosque, the town grew up. This was already a busy thoroughfare when the Arabs founded the Medina ('the town') in 698, leaving their mark in the form of a specifically Muslim urban pattern well suited to the economy of an Islamic society.

How a Medina is made up

Islamic urban and rural communities are organised on quite different lines. The character of a town depends on the main occupations of the people. Regardless of size, nothing is more unlike a village in the Sahel than the Medina; a rural centre might even have a larger population, but would still lack urban characteristics.

Depending on local conditions and methods of cultivation, people in the country may live together or isolated, be nomadic or sedentary; a wide range of dwellings from tents to permanent houses includes huts made from branches, *gourbies* (shacks), and *douars* (encampments).

There was no steady development or transition, such as took place in Europe, from rural village to urban organisation. The urban community links religious life and political power in a very characteristic way. A Medina will include the following: the Great Mosque (Jemaa); other mosques *(mesjeds)*; holy men's shrines *(zaouia)* and private cemeteries *(tourba)*; Koranic schools *(kouttabs* and *medersas)*; public baths *(hammams)*; washing places *(midhas)*; fountains *(massassas)*; *souks* (markets) and *fondouks* (hostelries); ramparts and gates.

Jacques Berque defines a medina as the town 'iron above', a 'centre of culture and faith'. Its social structure is strongly hierarchical: great landowners, political and military dignitaries, men of law and religion, craftsmen and traders, soldiers, and the common people. This hierarchy is reflected in the housing.

The town, P. Georges suggests, continues the countryside in the sense that it concentrates the wealth that the agricultural world produces but, as Berque points out, the threefold order of study, trade and handicrafts which characterises a medina is never found in a village. Urban and rural communities are differently organised to meet the requirements of different social groups. The life style of its inhabitants

Typical architecture in the Medina

tends to intensify the specifically urban features of a medina, while rural communities, however large, can never escape the centrifugal effects of the agricultural way of life.

Stages of the Medina's development

From the seventh century to the tenth, the Medina grew up around the Mosque of the Olive Tree. According to historians, a dozen smaller mosques were the starting point of new quarters – the mosque is the catalyst of urbanisation. There were five gates in the city walls.

Two suburbs developed, to the north and to the south, during the eleventh century. The Medina, now recognised as the capital, began to take final shape, while the suburbs continued to grow. At the end of the fourteenth century, the town looked very much as it does today. There were no further radical changes. Modifications were of course made to adapt the city to the needs of an ever-changing community, but the basic pattern was not affected.

When the French Protectorate was established in 1881, the centre of the Medina covered some hundred hectares, surrounded by ramparts and flanked north and south by two suburbs (Rbat Bab Souika and Rbat Bab Dzira), each with its own fortifications. The total urban area, covering 308 hectares, had 120,000 inhabitants, including 20,000 foreigners.

The Medina in 1881

The town plan drawn up by Colin in 1860 shows very clearly the contrast between the Medina and the surrounding countryside. It stood alone on the hill of Tunis, following the hill's contours. The Medina *was* the town, taking in the whole population of Tunis, including the foreigners in their own compound: there is no city but Islam as there is no God but Allah.

The roads from the city gates led almost immediately into the countryside. Trading went on at the gates and in the *fondouks,* while wheat, oil, olives and other harvested crops were garnered in the storerooms of the great houses. The town was a huge warehouse for the produce of distant estates.

The Bedouin had no place in the city except in the *oukala* (lodging house) or the *fondouk.* Bedouins came only to buy what they could not find in their local *souk* or village. Rural and urban were closed and separate worlds, meeting only to trade. Divorced from its hinterland, the town was completely closed in on itself.

The great Mosque called to prayer on Fridays and was the seat of learning; enclosed among the *souks,* it was like a heart controlling the ebb and flow of the city's life. From here, main thoroughfares branched out through the residential areas. Streets branching off from the main thoroughfares in turn enclosed groups of private houses situated on blind alleyways. These groups were quite separate from the public life of the main thoroughfares, on which were situated religious buildings *(mesjeds, medersas, zaouias, tourbas, kouttabs)*, or public buildings *(hammams, midhas, fondouks,* baking ovens).

Along the main thoroughfares, the social rhythm of everyday life was organised: the baths, the prayers in the *mesjed,* the homily in the *zaouia,* work in the *fondouk* or *souk,* study in the *kouttab* and the *medersa.* Off this beaten track, in the patios of the residential area where family life was carried on, the rhythm of life was quieter.

It is important to know something about this background not only because the monuments are important nationally and for mankind, but because of the accompanying way of life which could serve as a model in conditions of rapid urbanisation and economic underdevelopment. Not, of course, that planners should try to recreate medinas artificially; but if, despite planning and advanced technology, and as modern architects find it so difficult to satisfy elementary living conditions, it is surely worth taking a look at a model which, in its own day, could comply with the four principles laid down in the Athens Charter.

For if contemporary society is entitled to shape its own organisation, we should be able to tell planners what kind of living space we want.

As indicated above, the choice of site, the particular way in which the population was grouped, the physical make-up of the town, and its different stages of growth all contributed to a Muslim style of town plan that resulted in a medina. There has been no radical change in the make-up of a medina, or in the type of dwellings, in recorded history. This accounts for the traditional character of the town, reflecting a social structure that is itself deeply rooted in tradition. The organisation of craftsmen into guilds, for example, in *souks* and *fondouks* in well-defined areas, dates back to the foundation of the city of Tunis.

Before the advent of western-type town planning, accordingly, there was a traditional city, forming an indissoluble whole, in which each section of the population had its allotted place. This unity will be of importance in considering the question of rehabilitation.

The above account has deliberately avoided ideological considerations that arose during the colonial period. A passing reference may perhaps be made, however, to numerous writers who could see nothing in the Muslim town but disorder, confusion and squalor, and to the inept and disparaging comparisons made between the rectilinear Roman town and the Muslim model. Far from disappearing with independence, these preconceptions survive together with the over-simplified myth of an alleged conflict between tradition and modernity that makes it extremely difficult to defend the cultural values of the Medina.

Technicians, engineers and architects never learned to understand and appreciate the quality and economy of Muslim architecture and urbanisation; the Medina is dismissed out of hand as being archaic. However, a builder working in the town will not hesitate to deck a concrete slab out with a series of arches, for although the roofing method may be modern, he instinctively borrows from traditional architecture. Present-day Tunisian architecture thus becomes a pastiche. Even architects working on low-cost housing schemes fall for neo-colonial preconceptions: where traditional architecture could provide cheap housing, using local materials and methods, the models adopted will demand imported techniques and materials.

Decline of Medina 1881—1956

Side by side with the Muslim city, a new town was built on the orthogonal Roman plan between 1860 and 1956 in the political conditions of the colonial system. By 1956, there were thus two rival types of town on the site of Tunis, with marked contrasts in their use of building land, and a high degree of segregation.

The town that was a jumble of winding streets lost out to the other which was rectilinear and hygienic; the Medina lost out to its colonial rival. P. Georges, wrote in *La Ville* (1952): 'The panorama seen from the tower of the Mosque is as confused as that of Damascus or any Arab town. A succession of flat roofs, furrowed by narrow streets and cul-de-sacs, obviously lacking a coherent street system, muffled sounds, a town apart'; similarly, Letourneau wrote in *Les Villes Musulmanes d'Afrique du Nord* (1957): 'Nothing is less like a Muslim town in the Maghreb than the rectilinear avenues of a Roman or modern town; in an aerial photograph, any Muslim town looks like a maze or labyrinth.'

As soon as a feudal community starts to change under the influence of external factors such as colonisation, there is an urban transformation — or perhaps, more accurately, a mutation, in the biological sense of a sudden variation in hereditary characteristics. (The word feudal is used here for want of a better; it does not really describe the Islamic phenomenon, there being no real analogy with European feudal societies.)

The Medina left behind after the disrupting impact of the colonial experience might be called a mutant. The mutation occurs when function and framework part company. The break in the homogeneity of the traditional urban pattern may be sudden or gradual; the once indissoluble whole of the Medina split up into its constituent parts — religious, artisan, residential, military — all of which lost

131

A souk in the Medina

significance as they ceased to be the only models to which the Muslim population happened to live.

The political, administrative and military functions of the old town were taken over by the new order, the new town which took over all authority. Decisions were no longer taken at Dar El Bey, but at the French Residency.

Long in a state of crisis, the traditional artisan economy was faced at the beginning of the nineteenth century with the challenge of a capitalist economy from outside. Competition from imported goods damaged but did not economically destroy the Medina. 'The traditional trades survived not only because they produced more cheaply but because they also represented a civilisation.[2]

As a place of residence, the Medina was abandoned by its leading citizens, and country people swarmed in. By 1925, the average middle-class Tunisian preferred a suburban villa to the Medina. But while, for him, leaving the Medina meant a step up in the social scale, moving into the old town was likewise a step up for country people. The influx was so great that, in 1946, the population of the Medina and its suburbs was estimated at 230,000, an enormous figure which implies densities of over 1,200 inhabitants per hectare in certain places.

There was a cultural change also, the European town exerting a growing influence on the Muslim population.

'But if the older people felt in their hearts that this other culture was more efficient than their own, and even if they chose to send their children to the new schools, they clung, officially and in public life, to the past; few sheikhs of the Zitouna still sent their children to the Zitouna, but they continued passionately to defend the old culture and institutions.'[3]

Finally, the religious function was monopolised by traditionalists who were out of favour in the current political situation: the city is no longer the city of God. The new urban conception was a challenge to the Muslim urban unity and homogeneity; the Medina had become merely a residual urban element, its traditional character transformed and profoundly changed.

The way in which Tunis was split up into zones clearly reflected the underlying antagonisms and the social and racial segregation. There were conflicting social interests: the dominant French (and Italian) colonial interests; those of the leading Tunisian landowners; those of an emergent Tunisian middle class interested in business and professional careers; those of an urban proletariat in conditions of colonial expansion; those of rural migrants trying to adapt themselves

to the town; those of ethnic and religious minorities protected
by the colonial power. All these divergent interests meant that, in
1956, Tunis was a backward town, bewildered by the
contradictions inherent in colonialism, incapable of offering its
inhabitants a stable socio-economic future.

Under these conditions, there seemed no future for the Medina but
to shrink away, the loss of its traditional functions being the
inevitable outcome of the conflict in development as between the
Arab and the European towns.

Further deterioration, 1956-1970

As soon as Tunisia became independent, the middle classes virtually
deserted the Medina, their place been taken by still more migrants
from the countryside. By 1968, only 35 per cent were still Tunisian
middle class as against 65 per cent of people who had moved in
from the country.[4] In a little over ten years, the social structure of
the Medina had radically changed.

Reasons for the exodus

On the eve of independence, the homogeneity of the patriarchal
family, large and hierarchical, sharing one traditional dwelling, was
on the point of breaking up; it was preserved only by the presence of
the colonial power.

The new political conditions, a new code of personal right and
obligations, the taking over of the administration by Tunisians, new
employment possibilities, and educational expansion soon led to the
replacement of the extended family by the family of parents and
children. The latter has adopted the social and cultural behaviour
introduced during the colonial period and assimilated by the ruling
classes: the hierarchical family is no longer compatible with the
new political freedom.

'The change to the smaller family is thus the main cause of the
migration. The traditional house which suited the patriarchal family
no longer suits the smaller unit. Economic emancipation breeds a
legitimate desire for comfort. To the young man now free of
paternal authority, the house and family he associates with all the
weight of traditional constraints are typical for him of a backward
and stagnant society.'[5]

Leaving the Medina, he accordingly installed himself in the European
town vacated by the colonial population, or helped to build new
residential quarters elsewhere. His exodus is facilitated by a policy of

134

slum clearance and building loans. In itself generous, this policy is one of the reasons why the Medina is being deserted by its traditional population. Under its building loan policy, 1958 to 1961,[6] the State encouraged the construction of new houses; the loans were paid back from the rent received from letting out rooms in the former homes. The clearance policy has actually increased the demand for housing; slum dwellers and rural migrants rent a room at a time in the houses and mansions of the Medina. It costs from 5 to 7 dinars[7] to rent one room without water, gas or electricity, so that a five to eight roomed house brings in a total rent of 25 to 26 dinars per month. 'Instead of being a place to live in, the traditional house is becoming an article of exchange.' This practice is more common in the central Medina, where there are many more mansions and middle-class houses than in the outskirts. It may be noted that the houses are sometimes divided up by the owners themselves, so that it is not only the rural migrants who are responsible for deterioration.

Decay into slum
Converted by the owner before letting in order to accommodate several households, or adapted by the new occupants to their mode of living, the traditional Medina house is in ways worse than a shack in the shanty towns. However wretched or precarious, the shack is at least functional and gives scope to the ingenuity of the builder; it is also reminiscent of the new occupants' former dwelling in a way in which a Medina house can never be. They are bewildered by a certain luxury in the town house which is meaningless to them. The patio, formerly a place where the family met and talked, becomes a kind of no-man's land where no one is at home. '*Oukalisation* occurs when no one owns the patio or open space because several families unrelated to each other are living in the same house.'[8] The term *oukalisation* means using a building as if it were an *oukala* or lodging-house by migrants from the country.

Proletarianisation
There is the additional factor that the newly-installed rural migrants in the Medina have much the same income level and standard of living as the people in the shanty towns; they depend mainly on minor trades that earn them 15 to 20 dinars per month (7 per cent), factory work (4 per cent), or crafts (6 per cent).[7] These social and occupational conditions, and the low standards of hygiene and nutrition, reflect the deterioration of the Medina to the condition of a slum. Like the population of the shanty towns, the rural population that moved into the Medina is a sub-proletariat. The landless peasant has become an unemployed town dweller. The shanty towns

of the capital grew from the pauperisation of the countryside which started with colonialism.

> 'Taking only the three staple products — cereals, oil, livestock — as basis for the calculation, the average annual income of some 12,000 families living by agriculture in the shattered Tunisia of the 1880s could not have been less than 400 gold francs (100,000 of today's devalued francs); this is at least three times the 1948 average income of 400,000 to 450,000 Tunisian peasants.' (Jean Poncet: *La colonisation en Tunisie depuis 1881*)

It may be noted that at the beginning of the three-year plan, the average annual income per head of population was assessed at 10 dinars, and that the planners aimed at increasing it fourfold. The rural influx does not only affect housing. The *souk* itself is duplicated in street vendors whose customers are poorer than those who go to shops.

There are also other economic consequences.

Some of the functions of the Medina survived colonialism for political reasons. These disappeared with independence, so that 1956, for all practical purposes, marked the end. The Medina was swamped by the rural influx. Only the traditionalists who rejected the new economic and cultural ideas stayed on. But their numbers are dwindling, and the values they cherish are disappearing with them. Nostalgia for the good old times remains: 'Where can you find nowadays the quality of what the craftsman produced?'

Craftsmen have largely disappeared. Of 16,000 to 20,000 at independence, only a few thousand remain. The Office National de l'Artisanat, set up in 1959, deprived them of such monopolies as remained. It set up workshops where the artisan has lost his creativity, since the article to be produced is designed in a drawing office. A large store in the middle of the new town only sells the products of this new craftsmanship, which has more in common with the factory than with the creator. Many of those who have not been recruited by the Office and have stayed on in the Medina work mainly for the type of tourists who will buy anything, shoddy goods that are valued only for the money they fetch, not the work that goes into them.

Some *souks* have become vast bazaars in which a few antique dealers search for the last specimens of genuine craftsmanship which are now collectors' pieces. The traditional Medina has vanished, swallowed up by the country; the rural influx has engulfed the very heart of the town. Yet things go on as if nothing had happened. The guilds continue to enjoy legal recognition although they have long since lost any economic significance.

136

The Rehabilitation Operation

Rehabilitation is necessarily a complicated operation because of the
importance of preserving the traditional character of the Medina,
despite its loss of functions and its physical deterioration.

The first necessity is to get a real grasp on the problem, to get rid
of various colonial and neo-colonial preconceptions, and work out a
compromise which will be acceptable to the conservationists and to the
modernisers. This implies making a full-scale analysis of all aspects
of the Medina, including its past and present history. These experimental
studies at critical points could provide useful guidance for both the
planners and the general public. The rehabilitation of the Medina
cannot be usefully considered in isolation from plans for the whole
urban area of Greater Tunis.

The main factors in the deterioration of the Medina itself have been:
the change in the population living in the old houses, the exodus of
former inhabitants and an influx of people from the countryside;
changes of built-up density in the urban area; the deterioration of
monuments and features of historic importance; the transformation
of a traditional economy. The problems involved are linked, and this
complicates tackling them on a sector-by-sector approach. For
example, a monuments policy is hampered from the outset by squatters,
and by legal difficulties raised by joint ownership.

Specific proposals for the Medina have to be considered in the
context of the five parts which go to make up the general outline plan
for the city of Tunis as a whole: plans for the protection of monuments;
urban renewal; land occupation; traffic; equipment.

Protection of monuments
A survey has determined what constitutes the historic quarters, and
provided an inventory of monuments. It defines sites, lists town-planning
or architectural restrictions, indicates the areas to be safeguarded in the
case of groups, and deals with the scheduling of individual monuments.

Urban renewal
Once the areas have been defined, the next step is to decide what form
renewal is to take. It has to reconcile the claims of the old town with
those of the new, and remodel the layout of areas where they overlap.

Land occupation
This covers the disposition of the residential areas and their population
densities; the axes along which social life is mainly organised; and the
areas devoted to production or manufacture and trading.

137

Traffic

The Medina is the only part of Tunis entirely reserved for pedestrians. Most development plans include ways of allowing motor traffic. If the Medina is to preserve its integrity, the motor traffic problem must be dealt with otherwise and outside the Medina.

However, since it is the economic and the geographical centre of Tunis, large numbers of employees and customers are moving in and out of the Medina all day. On the road which encircles it, the traffic is as heavy as on the major thoroughfares in the western part of the capital. And as everyone wants to own a car nowadays, there will no doubt be a substantial demand for parking space by inhabitants of the Medina within the next ten years. Any plan must cover these future as well as existing requirements. This would provide the Medina with the same standard urban amenities as the rest of the town.

But pedestrians must also be provided for and, where necessary, given priority over car traffic. The remodelling of the town to provide this priority, and also to improve the public transport facilities would help to break down the barriers between the old town and the new, and make it easier for the vast majority (who are not likely to be able to afford cars within the next ten years) to get around. The increase in the number of cars is in any case likely to be large enough to warrant consideration in plans for dealing with traffic and parking problems.

Equipment

The Medina is more densely populated and less well-equipped than the rest of the city. In terms of earnings, it is on the same level as the shanty towns. So complex are the socio-economic problems that, for practical purposes, the municipality thought it best to divide the city into two parts: the legitimate Tunis composed of the colonial and recently built quarters, and the illegitimate Tunis of the Medina and its adjacent areas. The no-problem areas were then properly equipped, while the Medina and the shanty towns were simply forgotten.

Clearly, if the Medina is to be rehabilitated, it must be brought into the general planning and programming; if it is to be safeguarded and protected, its facilities must be brought up to the same standards as prevail in the rest of Tunis.

The technical and administrative services for urbanisation set up in the colonial period are not adequate to cope with the present problems. The discrepancy must be made good by the political authorities, who must deal with all five aspects of the general rehabilitation operation that were set out above. The final decisions are for the local authorities and the State.

The complicated causes of the increasing deterioration of the

Medina should not be tackled by the uncoordinated and often incompatible procedures open to the Municipality, and the Ministries of Culture, Public Works, Lands, and so on. A Greater Tunis *(District de Tunis)* now legally exists and must now become a practical reality as well. Its approach to the rehabilitation of the Medina must be democratic, and recognise the right of the local community to preserve its history and benefit, to the greatest extent possible, from the scheduling and rehabilitation of the Medina.

It often happens that housing and employment policies that are tied up with renewal and renovation tend to be over-concerned with the tourist aspect, and with luxury housing and shopping. The result is less likely to be rehabilitation than accentuated segregation. The purpose of rehabilitation is not to restore the old urban shell for private ends, nor to arrange the snobbish return of the ruling classes, nor to transform mansions into business or tourist development headquarters, nor to conserve museum pieces for the aesthetic delectation of a minority. There is nothing wrong with these uses in themselves — tourist attractions, for example, may bring in a tidy income — but they must never be allowed to become the main purpose of rehabilitation.

Rehabilitation presupposes a firm political determination to designate the old town, the Medina, as a common heritage which the local and State authorities are prepared to safeguard as a matter of priority. In legal terms, ownership of the site is invested in the municipality by a decision which defines the inalienable rights of the community over the old town as an entity, but which grants long leases to private owners (otherwise, the local authority would find itself in the same position as any developer seeking to buy on a speculative and rising real-estate market). Strong powers of expropriation, efficient judicial machinery and financial support from the State are necessary for the success of what then becomes, in legal terms, a renewal project.

NOTES

1. F. Choay: 'Historie et urbanisation' in *Annales,* juillet-août 1970.
2. Marthelot, 1955.
3. Chedly Klibi: 'Culture et style de vie' in *Les Villes,* Ecole pratique des Hautes Etudes, 1958.
4. *Cf.* the Survey by the Town Planning Workshop of the Association for the Safeguarding of the Medina (AUASM).
5. AUASM, J. El Kafi: 'La gourbification de la Medina de Tunis, terme de la dégradation de la trame urbaine traditionelle'.
6. *Building loans 1958-1961,* Société Tunisienne de Banque, Tunis.
7. *Cf.* AUASM, Eckert: 'Rural exodus to the Medina of Tunis', 1970.
8. AUASM, Revault Cladel: 'Medina: l'oukalisation', mars 1970.

TUNISIA: THE ARTISANS OF THE MEDINA

Dominique Champault

By and large, while fully appreciating the positive side of the activities of the Office National de l'Artisanat, it is very difficult to talk of artisans when each worker is a specialist limited to making part only of the final product. Further, the work of the artisans in the Medina is only marginal to the work of the Office; they are really competitors for the same market. The loss of initiative and individual responsibility in mass-produced work would inevitably end by abolishing true craftsmanship. If craftsmanship in the Medina is to survive, arrangements must be made which will permit co-existence.

The Medina and the workshops should each have their reserved sectors. At the production stage, this would mean allowing the Medina a monopoly in the production of such items as the Office workshops do not also produce; avoiding competition by limiting production, and limiting both to the production of certain items; at the distribution stage, the Medina would itself sell, at its own prices, only the items it itself produced, while the balance of its products would be freely sold outside. In the Medina, as elsewhere, artisans must be given the moral support of knowing that they are not exercising a despised and dying craft, but are upholders of a civilisation, expressing one of its aspects. The artisan should be able to take pride in his work and have no sense of inferiority in relation to factory techniques. This spirit could be fostered if each craft had its leaders, chosen for their professional skills and a certain breadth of spirit. They could be encouraged in turn by talks with technologists, artists and ethnologists from Tunisia or abroad. The press, the radio and television could likewise encourage and enhance craftsmanship.

Further measures could be considered. For example, half a dozen artisans could be sent each year for study in a good Mediterranean or Arab centre; or there could be an annual competition for Tunisia's best workers during an Artisan or Folklore Week.

It may be noted that many artisans have only a work-place and shop in the Medina, but do not live there with their families. It should be possible for them to live in the Medina and feel fully at home there. Residence in itself gives a sense of social cohesion. Certain studies would have to be made before measures could be taken, but in any case, artisans might be given priority in the allocation of renovated quarters, or accommodation which falls vacant.

But the question is not only one of status. The artisan must be able to earn a reasonable living and support his family. A number of problems which are linked must be dealt with: sales outlets, professional organisation, financial questions. Inside the Medina, there should be spot checks on the quality of artisan products. This could be counterbalanced by the award of a quality seal, to be affixed to each item, which would quickly become known to Tunisian and foreign buyers.

Indirect aid

Various co-operatives could help the individual artisan — by the bulk purchase of raw materials; cash advances on delivery; and possibly with sales. The State should reserve a certain part of its orders: purchases for government services, embassies abroad, and the rapidly expanding hotel industry. Certain orders should be reserved annually for artisans who had distinguished themselves as workmen of the year. And the State should of course ensure that payments are made punctually.

It might be interesting to see why some leatherwork imported from Morocco sells better than the local product. Customs protection would also help. There does not seem to be any reason, for example, why much of the curtains and other fabrics used in hotels should not be made locally rather than imported.

Morally as well as financially, the artisan working on his own would be greatly helped by some lightening of his tax burden. There need be no falling off in revenue, if the relief was paid for by slightly increasing the amount payable by producers who employ staff and tend to be more industrial than artisan.

Direct aid

To counter bureaucracy, artisans should be well represented on any agencies set up to encourage artisan activities. They will very soon produce their leaders and organisers, capable of ably seconding Government plans.

Seen in isolation, crafts might seem scarcely able to pay their way, but they take on a completely different perspective if seen in relation to the tourist possibilities of a large city like Tunis. The tourist comes to see something different; and it is the Medina which differentiates Tunis from other cities along the Mediterranean, and the artisan who gives the Medina part of its distinctive quality. He can be directly aided by subsidies, an apprenticeship system, quality premiums, and collective or individual advances when sales are bad or during the dead season.

Professional Organisations

A professional organisation for artisans in the Medina should be co-operative, be run by the artisans themselves, operate according to regulations drawn up jointly by them and the administration, and be both aided and supervised by the State.

Three points may be noted.

a) The results of certain existing co-operative training schemes have been disappointing. The reasons for this apparent failure should be investigated. The inquiries should not limit themselves to the persons immediately involved, but look at the ethnological, economic and social factors of which the latter may be more or less unaware. After discussions with leading craftsmen, it might then be possible for the investigators to come up with practical recommendations.

b) Some of the stronger guilds already have their own strict codes which define how an apprentice becomes a qualified worker, then a master craftsman (with corresponding wage grading) and, finally, an independent boss.

c) A mutual insurance scheme, for each trade, or for all of them if number are not sufficient, should be obligatory, subsidised by the State, and progressively introduced to cover illness, accident, death, and a pension scheme.

Practical Suggestions

The prestige of Tunisian workmanship can be boosted in a number of ways.

1. In education. Suitable references in history manuals in primary, secondary and higher education. Manual instruction in popular arts and techniques in schools equipped to provide it.

2. Exhibitions in official premises or large stores in the bigger towns, with articles in the local press, visits by groups from schools, apprenticeship schemes, workers and peasants; talks and film shows. This kind of educational publicity might also be provided by a travelling exhibition, run by someone who knew how to make contact with the public. To be really effective, demonstrations should be illustrated by the tools used, texts, diagrams, photo sequences showing the different phases of the work, and so on.

3. An illustrated periodical. This should be widely distributed, and be open to ethnologists, historians, artists, and artisans who could write themselves or be interviewed. The periodical could provide liaison between the various branches of artisans, each perhaps having its own section.

Mixing perfumes in the Medina

4. Other publicity could include a poster and slogan competition (perhaps open to schools); a 'best-worker-in-Tunisia' competition; and the use of products themselves for publicity purposes, *e.g.* in public places, reception rooms in public buildings and so on, and as prizes for social and economic services rendered and in sporting competitions, presented by some leading public figure. A campaign on the above lines would serve many purposes — enhance the cultural consciousness of all classes in the population; maintain outlets inside the country; raise the status of artisans in the community; provide an inducement to new apprentices.

Export and Tourist Market

Objects produced by craftsmen can no doubt be offered for sale in shops in certain hotels, and each hotel itself should set an example by using Tunisian ceramics, copper, carpets, and so on.

It should not be forgotten that craft objects can also be offered as gifts on such occasions as official visits by the Government, international congresses, and visits by distinguished foreigners on economic or social occasions.

Export, properly speaking, is really feasible only under certain forms, such as sales exhibitions in large stores (fairly common in Paris), in museums or international exhibitions. The exhibitions should be backed up by articles in the press and in the growing number of periodicals devoted to art and culture.

A Pilot Project

The Café Mrabet was one of the first Turkish cafes set up in Tunis. It has recently been restored and it is now being proposed that it should be the centre of an artisan district. An old wall separates the garden of the Café Mrabet from a street with a double row of shops which formerly sold silk and brocades. Close by, a dozen other premises open on to a rectangular courtyard, with a fine colonnade. Here, artisans exercising such traditional crafts as leatherwork, inlaying, wood carving and painting could be installed, and work under the eyes of the public to whom they could sell their products directly. This would almost certainly be popular with foreign visitors and provide an inducement for other young Tunisians to re-establish the contract between the creative artisan and the critical public of consumers. This kind of thing has been done very successfully in Mexico, for example. Although it would no doubt be somewhat artificial to start with, success would depend partly on the artisans feeling that they were not just objects of curiosity but creators worthy of interest. The project as a whole could do much to show the feasibility or otherwise of giving the artisan back his former position, in the changed social and economic conditions of contemporary Tunisia.

No one wants to see the Medina as a kind of empty historic shell, devoid of life or any purpose other than the satisfaction of nostalgic sentimentality. Unless it has a function in the life of the community, it can lend Tunisia neither prestige nor economic benefit, direct or indirect. And prestige and economic success depend here on knowing and accepting the conditions on which they depend.

8.   IRAN: THE VITALITY OF ISFAHAN

M. F. Siroux

Isfahan had an economy and a way of life which hardly changed in centuries and, like so many other towns and cities, was taken unawares by the vast changes of the twentieth century. It has had to come to terms with modernisation. The population is growing. Industry is expanding. At the same time, it is a city unique in the quality of its sites and monuments which must be conserved, for Iran and for the world.

Strong views are held: the emotional — sometimes passionately emotional — feelings of the lovers of antiquity, and the more down-to-earth concerns of the technicians and modernisers. Between these a compromise must be found. If not actually welcomed, it must be at least acceptable to all.

Isfahan is a living entity, well known to the international tourist. What measures are necessary now to allow normal economic expansion, and yet safeguard and conserve the character that makes it unique?

The conflicts of antiquity never interrupted trade between the Near East and the West. In its celebrated fairs, the high Middle Ages distributed the luxury products of Asia, shrouding their origins in mystery. The great travellers, merchants and missionaries of the thirteenth and fourteenth centuries unveiled a little of the mystery, and were mostly greeted with incredulity. It was not until the seventeenth century that some more garrulous pioneers, traders and churchmen provided some real information in the West about Iran, and Isfahan in particular. And in the last century, impregnated as it was with romanticism, talented writers, in poetic descriptions, blazoned the name and many attractions of Isfahan everywhere.

The visitor is conditioned beforehand by the tales of the earlier writers, and the colourful, slightly melancholy, descriptions of their successors. Another less easily defined impression derives from a very distant past, and from the contemplation of indefatigable human effort continuing in the same place. This effort has survived a thousand vicissitudes and, though steadfast, was no enemy to variety and diversification.

An unusually unimpaired model of a particularly homogeneous civilisation, Isfahan now faces the universal change which tends to annihilate individuality. The still intact framework for this civilisation could be carried away and disappear forever.

In the Near East as elsewhere, some places seem predestined.

146

Isfahan is one of them. Situated on an arid plateau at the end of a long valley, the Isfahan plain is watered by the Zayandeh-rud river and provides an oasis similar to many in Central Asia. What makes it different is its geographical situation, at the crossroads of vital thoroughfares which linked it to Babylon, the Caucases, the Caspian Sea and India. The plain contains no remains of the artificial hills which indicated occupation in pre-historic times or earlier. And this may be because the hills themselves were gradually demolished for the organic matter they contained which was highly prized by farmers. The hills may have been levelled off, and used as sites for temples and fortresses. (This indeed may be the origin of the slight terrace on which the Jum'a Mosque now stands).

Natural routes crossed at Isfahan, the routes which were followed by the traders who spread civilisation and were also the itinerary of the great migrations. Along their interminable length passed the Indo-European tribes. Later, using the same passes, came the Assyrians, great amateurs of the renowed horses of the plateaus, to inhabit Isfahan.

The first references to the town date back some 2,500 years. Among the villages scattered around the plain, two, although independent, seem to figure as ancestors. Gabai, later successively called Djaiy and Charistan, was on the north bank of the river, where the road to Sharaz starts. The second, Yahudieh, a trading centre, took its name from a Jewish colony supposed to have been transplanted there by the Assyrian Emperor Nebuchadnezzar from Jerusalem which he had just destroyed. The two towns, three or four kilometres from each other, had different cultures. In the course of centuries, Yahudieh (by and large the area to the east around the Jum'a Mosque) became the stronger, and absorbed the surrounding villages. Little further change occurred until the period of the Safavid dynasty. When Shah Abbas the Great made Isfahan his capital in 1590, he did not disturb the remunerative activities of the old quarters, which then extended approximately to the Ali Mosque; for his great building plans, he chose the sparsely populated area, largely taken up with gardens or crops, that extended to the river.

Safavid Isfahan

During the eight and a half centuries between the Arab invasion and the first construction by Shah Abbas I, Yahudieh continued to expand. Houses decayed and were replaced by others like them; there was little hesitation in using better materials from more important buildings as they also fell into ruins. As the centuries passed, there naturally were differences, but the changes occurred almost imperceptibly. Thus, when

Shah Abbas selected Isfahan, it was a city still very much as it had been at the beginning of the thirteenth century. His own great achievements, and those of his successors, spared the ancient city, leaving it still well-preserved today — a medieval city with a large part added by Safavid dynasty.

The old city, where the artisans worked and the merchants traded, was a source of wealth. Although a great builder who did not hesitate upon occasion to raze to the ground, Shah Abbas was also a realist, and was careful not to touch this very heavily populated area; cutting into the old town would have been very unpopular with its inhabitants.

To the south the city consisted mainly of shops and warehouses, a market place and caravan-assembly area such as may be found on the edge of many Moslem towns. Beyond were the countryside and the great parks. His basic plan was to join up this vast space with the earlier city, and locate there residences for himself and his nobles, and accommodation for the new population he would bring in to stimulate the economy. Some see in his designs a reflection of the mystic idea of the foor corners of the earth, in a kind of chessboard in four sectors, its north-south axis being the Chahar Bagh, its east-west axis the river.

The entire north-east quarter was to be reserved for the royal parks and his palaces. In the north-west would rise the magnificent residences of the nobles and, beyond them, the dwellings of the people moved in from Tabriz. South of the river were settled the Armenians who had been transplanted from Djulfa in Ajerbaijan. Lastly, the south-east, beyond the Chahar Bagh, which terminated in the immense thousand-acre garden, was for the Guebres, Zoroastrians moved out of their former encampments at Djulfa.

This grandiose plan was carried out in two stages. During the first (from 1588 to 1612) military operations were absorbing the bulk of his resources. This was nevertheless the time of the enlargement of the Ali Qapu, the High Gate that gave access to the parks and future palaces, housed the chancellory and ministries, and contained the favourite apartments of the king; the building of the Sheik Lutfullah mosque; and the laying down of the Chahar Bagh, with its canals and pools, decorative terraces and gardens which separated the royal parks from the other quarter where the king was urging his nobles to build their residences. Participation was voluntary, but was it not better to be in the king's good graces than risk a resentment which sometimes proved fatal? One of the king's companions built the remarkable bridge of the thirty-three arches which connects the two sections of the avenue.

The second phase of the work began in 1611 and lasted till the king's death. War and conquest were over, and a stable economy allowed him

148

to realise his dreams of grandeur, his architects starting with the great Maidan-e-Shah square, the largest in the world. From the Ali Qapu, his people and soldiers could catch a glimpse of him, leader of Shi-ism and omnipotent potentate.

In 1616, the great north-south axis of the square acquired the monumental ornaments of the gate to the royal mosque (completed only in 1640, after the death of the king) and the entrance to the bazaar. The bazaar remains almost intact and is unique, with its network of galleries, intersections, *caravanserai, madrassehs,* mosques and ancient mills.

Protecting the Past

The guiding principle of the great king, a practical man and a religious leader, was to separate inhabitants very different in origin, class and religion, without being overconcerned about the connections between them, and to locate the seat of the dynasty where it should be, in a central position among them.

Preserving the past and ensuring its integration into a modernised city involves the principal sectors to different degrees, and we can confine ourselves to three major sectors: the old town; the bazaar and Maidan-e-Shah; and the area of the parks and palaces. Even here, we can ignore many of the great monuments, including Chihul Sutun, Haft-Behesht, Ali-Qapu and the galleries of the Maidan, which are well on the way to restoration. The city is spreading out in all directions: industrialisation east and south, a new airfield to the north, new housing in the rural west. Hence there are the new traffic problems. The population is growing by natural increase, and immigration from the countryside.

The young working population in the old quarters demands modern hygiene, modern working conditions, proper housing and brighter premises that open on to wide streets. There is no going back on this, and whole quarters have been abandoned as a result. Buildings in clay will last a century if well maintained, but as soon as serious problems arise, major repairs may cost more than rebuilding. Many old buildings are interesting, and worthy of preservation, but new uses must be found for them. Public services badly need improving, private interests have to be dealt with, and speculation curbed. The questions of modern urbanism will have to be discussed with sociologists, archaeologists, the tourist organisations, economists, and financiers.

Isfahan is a flat city whose features have for two millenia maintained the same traditional appearance, with here and there superb monuments that have survived. It is a symbiosis which illuminates the medieval mind, when religion, learning, work and living formed an indissoluble whole — as they did in the Middle Ages in the West, which we should understand better if the old quarters surrounding cathedrals and monuments had not been ruthlessly destroyed. Except for palaces, or commemorative monuments which founders wished to make sacred by isolating them, it was never the intention of benefactors, in demonstrating their fervour or charity, to keep aloof from humanity of which they were a part. The same feeling is still miraculously intact at Isfahan. To preserve it, monuments and their surroundings must not only be restored, but kept authentically alive. The population must agree, and must never have the humiliating impression of constituting an artificial 'reserve'.

So, the old quarters must be modernised. Fortunately, none of the obstacles are insurmountable. The social problem is basic. The residents are not, in general, wealthy. The younger people value better accommodation and working conditions, and will understandably move elsewhere to get them. The only way to prevent them moving is by offering improved living conditions, work-places, and public services where they are.

Repairs are less of a problem than their financing. Owners often have little money; much of the repair work must either be subsidised or entirely paid for by the community, which must also pay the costs of reconstructing sections of the bazaar and the covered alleys. Houses built on family or purchased sites will increasingly raise the question of building permits and property speculation. Strict but intelligent controls governing facades and zones adjoining the new avenues will no doubt be necessary.

Traffic, parking, drainage and electrification are related problems. In many places, bottlenecks could be reduced without much difficulty by cutting walls. Asphalting would prevent the clouds of dust in summer and mud in winter; rain may be rare, but often comes in a deluge which demands better drainage facilities. Many streets could be one-way, especially in areas which are at present nothing but rubbish dumps, beyond redemption. These latter could, where necessary, be enclosed and provide detours, parking places, or green spaces in areas in which they are particularly lacking.

Over the centuries, the level of streets and roads has risen — sometimes a metre or more above the level of the adjacent courts and houses; the latter, indeed, are often in hollows created where clay was removed for ramparts and other great constructions of the past. This causes major problems in linking up with the drainage system that is being built — itself complicated by the flatness of the city site. The use of trenches, which require frequent emptying, should be completely abandoned. In many places the use of collecting tanks (which could be put underground, in waste plots of ground) will

150

Courtyard of madresseh

151

be inevitable. The less expensive solution of common cesspools for several houses may be employed, provided they are supervised by the public services.

Rain-water should be evacuated under pressure into deep permeable soil (as has been done for over a hundred years in some provinces in France). Piped drinking water is being installed. This programme is being speeded up. Incidentally, it should not overlook the provision of supplies to the much-used public fountains.

Moslem cities are made to look extremely discreet, if not positively secretive by long lines of blank walls, and solid doors, sometimes with decorative locks. Old Isfahan has kept this appearance, although varied by clay coverings and the bluish reflections of plaster facings. These are tending to disappear, but should be repaired and preserved by applying similar, more solid facings.

Streets could be made more pleasant, at certain intersections, by planting single plane trees: those we still admire, now enormous, were planted centuries ago. Why not, as in the past, use tiny plots to plant these trees, so perfectly suited to the climate?

In the old quarters renovated buildings will induce people to stay. Some may seek work elsewhere, in factories or offices in the new zones, going by minibus to the car parks, or travelling by regular buses along the new avenues. Others will choose to be artisans. For, although traditional crafts are declining, industrialisation is promoting new skills, and making demands that can be satisfied by small family industries producing such items as accessories, or surgical instruments; the skills and manual dexterity of the Iranians are well-known.

Life in towns requires many buildings for public use — kindergartens, primary and technical schools, dispensaries, cultural or entertainment halls, gymnasia, and so on. With minor alterations, these could fairly easily be installed in restored buildings. The old town also contains many mansions that have come down in the world. It should not be difficult to interest families with money in the houses of their ancestors — here where Shah Abbas himself lived for many years.

Immediate Measures

The main streets and roadways of Isfahan are already there, and little can be done about them except by such local improvements as touching up façades or creating little squares.

Something must be done at once about monuments of historical or aesthetic quality, without prejudice to the complete restoration which may have to be held over until later. Something must similarly be done in the old town, in combination with modernisation to the extent of providing water, sewers and electricity.

The sector to the north of the Safavid town must be scheduled and safeguarded, in addition to the work of restoration and consolidation which is taking place in the Safavid town itself (Ali-Qapu; Chihil Sutun; Haft Behesht; Shah-e-Maidan). The northern sector is also unique, with its bazaars, *caravanserai, madrassahs,* hammams, and so on; the Monuments Service has almost completed its detailed survey of the sector.

The work of renovation must be very carefully thought out beforehand. Surveys will form the basis of a programme which will depend partly on the state of the sites and the classification of the monuments (some are religious property, others are in private hands) and partly on the manner of financing (undertaken by the State, or subsidised by it). Account will also have to be taken of the uses to which monuments, once renovated, can be put — public or social uses, or trade.

The very first task will be to put back vaulted roofs in bazaars which have fallen in. This need not respect their original design, as they have been often repaired and reconstructed during the last three centuries. The main thing is to restore the former effect of these long, covered galleries, now often interrupted by makeshift wooden structures. Similarly, something must also be done immediately about temporarily buttressing or propping up the framework of many monuments, paying special attention to the infiltration of water and the undermining of the sub-foundations. Full restoration can come later.

Some restoration could be undertaken at once, *e.g.* the Royal Caravanserai, which has been adequately surveyed, and which could be faithfully reconstructed from the considerable remains that are still there. It is quite close to the Maidan-e-Shah, and could be made into a hotel for young tourists.

The old town:

a) *From the Bazaar to the Jum'a Mosque.* This takes in all of the Harun-e-Velayet, and the Ali Mosque and Minaret. Constructions along the way need maintenance, and such ugly modern additions as corrugated iron shutters and sheds should be eliminated. The adjoining, ugly Maidan-e-Qadim, where a cotton trade is carried on, needs to have its façades renovated, and would be improved by some trees.

b) *From the Jum'a Mosque to Darb-e-Iman.* This takes in all of the Jum'a Mosque area, and is very varied. It is much used by tourists, and even more so by the inhabitants. The visitor passes through two bazaars (where the arched roofs need consolidation); reaches the high gateway of the Dar Dasht minarets; and sees the Agha Nur Mosque, a *caravanserai* which is also Qajar and could easily be

153

A facade of the caravanserai (May 1972)

154

re-adapted, and Darb-e-Iman, famous for its outer coverings, which is one of the rare buildings having three courtyards (which like the west façade, need repairing). A renovation scheme would involve the restoration of the walls along the way, and the end portions of alleys and *cul-de-sacs*. Care must be taken that the electrification of the area does not disfigure certain façades such as the Dar Dasht minarets.

The two sectors must mentioned, in the old town, form part of the first priority programme. Two further groups might be added to them.

c) *The Chaya Mosque and the Imam-zadeh Ismael.* This is a small group dating from different centuries, with a *madrassah* courtyard and a Chahar Su. The group and courtyard have been restored, but could be still further improved, and the Chahar has been consolidated somewhat, but the charming courtyard needs renovation. Care must then be taken to preserve the immediate surroundings, including a lateral street, with an old plane tree that once sheltered a watering point which is now walled up. The wall surrounding the very old cemetery should be replaced by a light barrier, in order to open up the view on the dome of the Iman-zadeh which, with the Mosque, are close to Hatef Avenue, and quite accessible.

d) *Tomb of Baba Kasem.* Similar measures should be taken in regard of the tomb and the area between it and the Enami *madrassah*.

Renovation of the old town

Old Isfahan is so extensive that it would seem foolish to hope to preserve everything.

However, to the quarters and sectors already mentioned, others should be added: the area around the Hakim and Sorkhi Mosques in the Gol-Bahar; and the approaches to the Darb-e-Kushk and the Seyyed Mosque in the Mahalleh-Now quarter. Care should also be taken of various fountains, picturesque road-crossings, and so on.

But the population is growing, and major reconstructions are being carried out to meet its growing needs — in the Joobareh and Yaz-abad quarters for example. Such expansion is bound to continue, so that the only reasonable policy is to channel it in such a way as to preserve an essentially Iranian character. In other words, the official services must lay down regulations and give instructions to be respected in particular renovation schemes; and this in turn implies confidence on both sides. It is clear from the topographical survey that certain narrow thoroughfares could be widened without serious difficulty at points where they are really much too narrow. Some streets could be designated as one-way, and parking spots provided at places which are beyond repair. If there have to be new roads, there is no reason why they should not be straight. Filling in may also be necessary, as internal courtyards are often much lower than the roads and cause drainage problems.

Electricity is being brought to the old quarters — reasonably enough in the simplest and cheapest way, by overhead lines. The result, unfortunately, is not picturesque, and is particularly out of place near some monuments. At such points, measures should be taken immediately to have the mains put underground, even if this costs somewhat more.

Materials and colours used in new buildings in some of the areas mentioned often clash with their surroundings. Gates giving on to streets are amongst the worst offenders. Recommendations and models issued with the building permit might help to check over-exuberant imaginations.

In the renovation of religious and other buildings, too much use is made of white, strictly calibrated industrial bricks. The material is too different, and clashes with the general colour of the old quarters, which is mostly pinkish ochre. There is no difficulty in finding brick prepared in the old way, and keeping the others for modern building programmes in the outskirts of the town. Such trees as planes and willows should be planted here and there, as they formerly were at street corners, near fountains.

A maximum height should be specified for buildings. Such special cases as water towers should be considered separately, so as to avoid blots on the view.

The centre of Isfahan has long had its wide avenues, but certain changes have become necessary in the Maidan-e-Shah, and the quarters leading on to it.

The Maidan is immense — 520 x 120 metres. It had many purposes, being used, *inter alia,* as a polo-ground, a meeting place, a military parade ground. The creation of a garden some forty years ago prevented it from being split up. The general perspective was saved, except where the Sepah and Hafez Avenues led in to it. These are very busy streets, carrying most of the east-west traffic, with a great deal of parking around the bazaar area.

There would be no major technical difficulty in restoring the façades affected by the two avenues and the street of the coppersmiths. The parking problem could be dealt with by using the ground sloping downwards north of Hafez Avenue for a two-level garage. This site has no visual interest, and is at present anarchically used. The through-traffic could be limited to tourist care only, larger vehicles being diverted.

An underground passage under the Maidan would not be a feasible solution. Apart from the heavy cost, it would have to go to a depth of 7.5 metres to accommodate lorries, and also have long access ways. Ground water would cause waterproofing problems, in addition to ventilation and drainage difficulties; and there would always be the possibility of traffic incidents in such passages, causing bottlenecks, inside and out.

It is quite possible to create or recuperate more free space around the Maidan, by suitable programming and by arranging that hotels or buildings used for cultural purposes are built low, with due regard to their surroundings and the desirability of keeping as much green space as possible. The Chahar Bagh and the area between the river and the Shah Mosque involve several problems. This is a vast area which formerly constituted the imperial parks, with pavilions and ornamental ponds; gardens and fairly extensive properties still subsist. The role of the Chahar Bagh itself has completely changed. The former picturesque promenade, with its gardens, gates and belvederes, has become an increasingly busy road, full of every kind of business which has meanwhile transferred there.

At first sight, it would seem possible to provide a major east-west thoroughfare south of the Shah Mosque. This would ease the traffic crossing the Maidan. But shops would have to be completely forbidden along the sidewalks, and trees provided instead. It would become obligatory to use part of the site for gardens only, and the building density would have to be strictly limited. The road would have to wind a little, and would end at a small square formed at the Chahar Bagh.

Rather than create a large thoroughfare more or less parallel to the Chahar Bagh in an area with little building, and stretching from the present Town Hall to the river, it would seem possible to appropriate enough land to enlarge the west road parallel to the Chahar Bagh. It starts at the Fine Arts School and ends at the Maidan. It could be continued north to the Reza Shah Pahlavi Avenue. It was inevitable that the first road, through an area that was still green, would attract businesses; sooner or later, restrictive orders and regulations are defied as a result of the pressures of commercial expansion and speculation.

Taking in both sides, the proposed road west, depending on where it is decided to end it, would be either 2.4 or 4 kilometres long. There are no major monuments, and business streets which would link it up with the Chahar Bagh could be allowed to develop there.

The Timing of Various Operations

1. It is very urgently necessary to safeguard the old quarters listed above, *i.e.* the area north of the Maidan-e-Shah and the priority streets and groups. The various monuments, bazaars and so on should be listed without delay, indicating, where appropriate,

157

proposed alternative uses.

The second operation should be the consolidation, by props and buttresses, of the parts worst affected; the third a methodical restoration, with due regard to any new uses (*e.g. caravanserai* adapted for use as a hostel or offices). There is no reason why, meanwhile, work on the vaulted roofs on the bazaars, the Royal Caravanserai and so on should not at the same time be speeded up.

2. Great care must be taken to prevent abusive and uncontrolled demolition in the old quarters, and especially in the streets mentioned above. In densely-inhabited areas, whether or not frequented by tourists, any reconstructions must be carefully supervised. State subsidies should be provided to encourage the modernisation of dwellings which can be quite satisfactorily repaired (mostly roofs and lower foundations).

In all these various operations, the friendly and willing co-operation of the parties concerned is absolutely essential.

3. The proposed new streets or roads in the old town and in the Safavid quarter (Chahar Bagh, area south of the Jum'a Mosque) should be dealt with in an urgent programme, drawn up by commissions where the views of all interests dealing with town planning (including those of the lawyers) can be co-ordinated.

4. We are not concerned here with new town planning in the industrial and outlying areas. It may be stated, however, that care must be taken to avoid planning new avenues in such a way as to add further to the congestion in the centre of the town.

A Joint Effort

Times are changing very rapidly. How can a city, old, beautiful and unique, keep all that makes it unique, and still allow its inhabitants to keep pace with a changing world? The unexpected difficulties which are nevertheless bound to crop up and could spoil everything can only be avoided by involving the whole community, and by an impartial and well-coordinated policy.

This could best be achieved by a kind of general staff, headed by someone who is well aware of all the issues (historical, aesthetic and technical) which could meet regularly and call upon representatives of the various interests involved (*e.g.* the roads, traffic, drains, water, electricity services; the Historical Monuments Department; owners and residents, juridical authorities; and so on). This general staff, which would prepare the programmes, would have to be backed by a permanent office whose documentation would be open to all. It would have to have powers to ensure that its decisions and instructions were respected in word and spirit.

9.   ITALY: THE OTHER VENICE

Mario Rinaldo

In the sixth century AD, in the mud flats of the Venetian lagoon, a town was founded on some islands in the Alto River as a refuge from barbarian invaders. With time and industry, tempered with adversity, a maritime mercantile empire developed. At its height the city was acknowledged to be one of the great powers of Europe and wealth poured into it.

The mansions and palatial structures which were built reflected several architectural traditions. They were graced with frescoes and hung with works of art created by the leading artists of the Renaissance, making scholars in general and the goal of millions of visitors.

Today the city is in part a museum, but it is also a place where people live, work, shop — it is a community. The world knows the Venice of St Mark's Square, of the beautiful and decaying palaces of the Grand Canal, but is less aware of the permanent core of the city with its year-round inhabitants.

The casual visitor, usually going to Venice between April and October, has the impression that the city throbs with life. With the end of the tourist season, however, many of the hotels, restaurants and shops close, and it is soon evident that even many of the people who are employed there are seasonal transients. With the coming of winter one can see the permanent inhabitants of the city and, year by year since about 1950 their numbers decline.

Other demographic changes have been taking place. The historic city is becoming a place for people too old or too poor to change. It is losing its middle and upper classes and, unless this tendency is arrested, only its palatial buildings will be preserved as a museum and it will no longer be a living community.

The implications of these changes have been carefully studied in a detailed survey in 1969 of living conditions in the old city. The results of the survey speak for themselves.

Between 1951 and 1961, years of recent census-taking, the population of island Venice dropped from 191,199 to 153,512, at an annual rate of 2.2 per cent (island Venice denotes the historic centre plus the islands of the Giudecca, Murano and Burano). By the end of 1969 it was 127,819 representing a new annual decrease of 2.3 per cent. This makes a total decrease over eighteen years of 63,380, which is equal to more than two thirds of the present population of Treviso (89,267) and larger than that of Rovigo (48,425) or Belluno (34,129)—towns of the province of Venetia. The main factor in the decrease has been the mass exodus from the centre to the mainland.

The population of the commune of Venice as a whole has always shown an increase: it was 316,891 in 1951, 347,347 in 1961 and 367,631 at the end of 1969. But whereas, before World War II, the increase of population was fairly uniform over the whole commune, about 1950 the position changed and, from then onwards there was a high rate of increase on the mainland, a moderate increase along the estuary and a pronounced decrease in the historic city centre itself. In 1951, 60.3 per cent of the total population of the commune lived in the historic centre; this percentage had dropped, by 1961, to 44.2 per cent, and by 1969, to only 34.7 per cent.

The decrease in the population of the historic centre of Venice has been due to two factors: natural (birth and death rates) and social (migration). Central Venice in the past three years has had a birth rate of 12.9 per thousand and a death rate of 13.5 per thousand, *i.e.* a minus total, as against 16.9 and 9.5 respectively — a plus total — for the commune as a whole. While the birth rate has remained roughly constant, the death rate has shown an increase.

As regards migration: 145,696 people emigrated from the city centre between 1951 and 1969, while only 78,897 people immigrated — making a total loss of 66,709 people and an annual average of 3,511.

The most striking feature of the demographic situation in recent years, after the major exodus of the period 1951-61, which was due to the dearth of employment in the historic centre of Venice, has been the increasing impoverishment of the population. Now this must be attributed to causes other than the employment situation. There are now far more jobs in the centre of Venice than can be filled by the local population; thus large numbers of workers commute to the centre from the surrounding areas.

The number of jobs available in the centre of Venice, in the period between 1951 and 1969, was always in the region of 61,000 to 63,000; whereas the number of available workers, *i.e.,* those engaged in productive work or capable of undertaking such work, fell from 71,000 in 1951 to 59,000 in 1961 and to 44,000 in 1969. A survey made in 1964 showed that the number of people commuting *to* Venice to work exceeded the number commuting *from* Venice by 12,000. This figure has now risen to 17,000. Approximately 70 per cent of this traffic is between the mainland and central Venice.

The main reason for the loss of inhabitants is no doubt the acute shortage of adequate housing in the centre. At the time of the last census in the historic centre there were 37,597 housing units, containing

160

145,255 rooms, occupied by 141,944 persons; 1,126 units, containing 7,376 rooms, unoccupied; and 377 units, classed as unfit for habitation occupied by 1,113 persons. Thus the average number of people per room, for the flats occupied, was less than one, *i.e.* 0.98.

Since, in the period 1961-69, the population of Venice decreased by 25,693 and, in the same period, the housing available increased by 1,413 units, containing 5,824 rooms, the average number of persons per room has now dropped to 0.8 per cent, a figure which compares favourably with that of the principal Italian urban centres.

The Quality of Housing

When it comes to the question of the quality of housing, however, the situation is entirely different; the island has little available space on which suitable new housing can be built. This, combined with the fact that little has been done to restore old houses, has produced a marked and growing discrepancy between housing conditions in Venice and those in the newer urban centres which have steadily improving standards.

A special survey was made to compare housing in Venice with those prevailing in other towns of Italy. The gravest shortcomings relate to sanitation, heating, damp and the general state of preservation. It was ascertained that, out of a total of approximately 39,400 dwellings in Venice between 17,000 and 19,000 dwellings require drastic renovation and repair.

Only a small proportion of the total housing is unoccupied (*i.e.* in 1970, 1,600 units, of which 810 are in the process of renovation and will come on the market; over 300 have been taken over for other purposes, 200 are uninhabitable).

Ground-floor flats number more than 4,600, of which less than 700 belong to the public authorities. At least two thirds of these are unsuitable for habitation; and it is possible that eventually the general policy will be to use none of them for living. The ground-floor flats covered by the survey are occupied by about 13,500 people, nearly all of modest means; 60 per cent of them expressed a wish to leave these premises.

Of a total of about 37,800 occupied flats, 11,900 are lived in by the owners, 13,500 let at controlled rents, 11,200 let at uncontrolled rents, and 1,200 occupied on other terms. These figures reflect a serious shortage of accommodation on the market: it is clear, merely from the statistics of marriages celebrated in the historic centre of Venice, that there must be a potential demand for more than 1,100 dwellings a year.

Of the 13,500 dwellings let at controlled rents, 4,100 belong to

'Not much room for play' Venice

the public authorities, 9,200 to private individuals and about 200 to private companies. There are 38,000 people in premises they own, 41,500 in controlled rent premises, 37,000 in uncontrolled rent premises and 3,500 under other arrangements.

The most recent population trend has further increased the number of people commuting to work in Venice: 22,000 coming to Venice as against 5,000 going from Venice to work elsewhere. These commuters consist mainly of medium and small wage-earners, independent workers and white-collar employees. They include very few of the better paid workers in the managerial of professional category and relatively few of the less highly paid, such as manual workers. (The inhabitants of Venice include a large proportion of people in the high income brackets and relatively few in the intermediate brackets.)

Over a third (44,000) of the people now living in Venice want to move from their lodgings, nearly all these because of the unsatisfactory condition of their dwellings. However, 38,000 of these intend to go on living in Venice proper. There are 3,000 who intend to leave the centre who would stay if they could get satisfactory housing.

Therefore it may be deduced that: the standard of housing in Venice is very poor; and, to remedy the situation at least 18,000 dwellings would have to be renovated. Some 58,000 people, most of them in the low-income bracket, live in poor quality housing; while most of the people now living in Venice would prefer to continue living there.

When providing housing, the main emphasis has always been on building new houses, often of questionable quality, rather than on repairing existing ones.

Early Planning and Projects

In the 1891 general redevelopment plan for the Commune of Venice, the industrial centres were located inside the city: relations between central Venice and the mainland were functional and were maintained by the rail and water transport facilities then existing. This plan provided for major construction projects: the building of seaward dikes designed to re-establish Venice as a port, and the erection of cheap housing in zones not yet built on.

In the years after World War I, with the establishment of Porto Marghera, a new conception emerged, still hinging upon the historic centre – the tourist aspect of which was accentuated – with extension of work on the mainland. Legislative provision was made for establishing both the industrial zone and the residential part of Marghera and building the motor-causeway across the lagoon. But it was not until 1939 that the 'Preliminary project for the renovation of the historic centre of Venice' was produced; it suspended plans for cheap housing in zones hitherto not built on, and restricted grants for the renovation of existing housing to a few special cases.

However, the 1961 general preliminary project paid special attention to the industrial, residential and tourist development of the mainland and the estuary, hardly touching the historic centre of Venice. It glossed over the problems of the renovation of housing in the centre.

Housing has been very much affected by these shifts of attitude. One effect was the spread of cheap housing in the years after 1920; the subsequent policies have led to a worsening of the situation. Also detrimental has been the transfer of financial investment from property – from which the members of Venetian upper classes derived their income – to industry. Most Venetian capital is now used outside the city centre, which of course, offers no possibilities for industrial investment. Little is spent on tourist development, but on Capital projects more remunerative than the costly improvement of Venetian housing with low profit. This trend was accentuated in the years followed World War II when the authorities were concentrating mainly on creating more employment in the centre of Venice – in the hope of slowing down the exodus. However, the migration was then, and still is, due mainly to the attractions exercised by the mainland with its cheaper and better housing.

The real problem was evaded – a concentration on the search for free space on which to build new housing. The most recent example is the construction in 1960 of housing on the island of Sacca Fisola, near the Giudecca.

As early as 1910 R. Vivante, in a survey *(Il problema delle abitazioni in Venezia* – 'The problem of housing in Venice', Venice 1910), while recommending the adoption of a law 'under which it would be possible to take over uninhabitable houses on payment of the value of the ground plus that of the building materials', wondered 'whether it would not be possible, with the ordinary expropriation machinery or, better, with machinery instituted under a new law, justified by the exceptionally serious situation of our city, to give the commune possession of certain areas which, ceded on reasonable terms to private persons, could be used for the large-scale erection of new houses to replace the old ones no longer habitable. If this were done, and private initiative were stimulated by additional tax relief . . . we would be able, within the space of a few years, to improve our housing and bring it much more closely into line with the special demands of our city'.

It is no longer possible today to find new open spaces on which there is no alternative except to renovate existing housing.

Account must be taken not only of financial considerations but

164

also of the preservation of the original character of the city and – first and foremost – its social structure. Such operations would affect areas containing a high percentage of controlled-rent houses, occupied by people of modest means; and any plans which failed to take account of that, and were swayed by commercial considerations, would inevitably cause a wave of speculation which would pauperise the population and further worsen the social composition problem.

Facts must be faced: investment in housing improvement can yield only a low return; and the present exodus can neither be halted nor reversed until central Venice is able to offer housing conditions comparable with those prevailing on the mainland and at similar rents.

Renovation must be given absolute priority; otherwise, the population of Venice will be reduced to a tiny, disparate community.

Plan of the 1969 survey

The unique configuration of Venice presents a considerable obstacle to classifying the quality of its housing. There is in fact no standard of comparison, nor can the housing be classified in absolute terms. Moreover, Venice is so built that there are often to be found, in one and the same edifice, premises utterly disparate.

It was decided in planning the 1969 survey that, after assembling facts for the study of housing, the survey would proceed by means of sampling.

All the housing units in Venice were divided into ten categories, according to number of rooms. One in every ten such units was taken from each category to serve as a sample – 3,936 in all. Their quality was ascertained through personal interviews, based on a sixty-two-item questionnaire covering the features of the premises themselves and of the building in which they were located, also the number and status of the occupants, and their desires in regard to other accommodation.

Housing was classified on the basis of lists drawn up for the 1961 population census. The number of new units constructed between the 1961 census and July 1969, when the survey was made, was only just over a thousand – thus not enough to invalidate the results obtained. Moreover, steps were taken to ensure that no interviews were missed.

A very large amount of information was amassed. The report pinpoints aspects that afford a clear picture of living conditions in the historic centre of Venice.

Of the 3,936 housing units covered by the survey, 160 (4 per cent) were unoccupied, 3,776 (96 per cent) were occupied by 4,126 families, composed of 12,251 persons. Thus, each unit is occupied on average by 1.1 families. As regards the number of inhabitants per unit occupied room occupancy, there has been a marked improvement since 1961 (0.86 per room as against 0.98). (A 'room' is defined as a space or area in a housing unit, having an outside window providing light and air, and large enough to accommodate at least one bed, leaving space enough to spare for one person.)

The steady exodus from 1962 to 1969 lessened overcrowding but not sharing. This confirms that most of those who moved out of Venice were young people, mainly people leaving their family homes. The average age of the population of central Venice is thirty-nine, against an average of thirty-two for the mainland. These figures on occupancy differ substantially from the average national figures which in 1961 showed 45.8 per cent owner-occupied, 46.6 per cent rented and 7 per cent other.

There is obviously a direct link between this situation and the high proportion of controlled-rent premises, which further confirms that the exodus from Venice has scarcely affected the older age groups.

It was found that for more than half the controlled rent premises the monthly rent, exclusive of any co-ownership charges, was at the time under 10,000 lires; and only 4.3 per cent over 30,000 lires. Of the uncontrolled rent category, the largest group was that paying between 10,000 and 30,000 lires; about one-third over 30,000 lires.

However, the persons interviewed were reluctant to state how much rent they paid, and tended generally to give a lower figure, particularly in the case of uncontrolled rents. The number of units with uncontrolled rents in excess of 50,000 lires per month appeared to be surprisingly small, and quite a number of rents stated as being between 30,000 and 50,000 lires were probably higher. None the less, over 50 per cent of the controlled rents were stated at less than 10,000 lires, and that is one reason why people are loath to move elsewhere, another being the reluctance to undertake repairs.

Little attraction for investment
The fact that private companies own so little property is indicative of their lack of interest in Venice; they prefer to invest in the new urban areas or in other real estate which brings bigger returns. More housing has been acquired by public authorities, in continuation of a policy adopted at the end of the last century. Conspicuous among public authorities is the *Istituto Autonomo Case Popolari* (Autonomous Institute for People's Housing) which, since 1899, has built large groups of housing, particularly in the Cannaregio, Dorsoduro and Santa Croce districts and on the Giudecca. This body, between the time when it was founded and 1967, built 2,731 flats, with a total of 9,172 living rooms. Other public authorities owning a large amount of property are the Commune of Venice and GESCAL.

A Venetian palace falling into ruins

This policy has played a decisive part in the reconstruction of the historic centre of Venice, although it has concentrated rather on meeting the quantitative demand for housing than on the renovation of existing buildings. But more than 77 per cent of rented houses belong to private owners. A recent survey shows that more than 92 per cent of Venetian house property owners own between one and four blocks only — according to Giuliano Segre, in *La Revista Veneta* (Venetian Review). Thus we find a considerable amount of public ownership alongside private ownership on a fairly small scale.

Some Findings of the Survey

One of the main objects of the survey was to assess the standard of Venetian housing, including the possession of specific features.

Type of entrance:
25.5 per cent have a separate entrance, 73 per cent a common entrance, and only 1.5 per cent a common entrance complete with porter's lodge. The flats having their own entrance reflect an old Venetian desire for a 'door of one's own' — often obtained by alterations which give a separate door, inconveniently placed inside the building. As regards inside entrances (to flats on a first floor or above) — 25.8 per cent are reached by an inconvenient staircase, 68 per cent by an ordinary staircase, 4.2 per cent by a wide, palatial staircase. Only 2 per cent can be reached by lift.

Distribution by floors:
A large proportion of flats are on the ground floor, larger than in 1910, when it was 10.5 per cent, according to a survey published by R. Vivante, excluding Murano and Burano. The increased proportion indicates that the ground floor is used for living premises even in houses built after 1910 (13,000 more houses were constructed than were demolished), despite the risk of flooding.

In studying the size of flats, it was found that 31.5 per cent had less than 60 square metres of useful surface area. In the next category, up to 80 square metres, were 32.9 per cent: up to 100 square metres, 16.8 per cent, and up to 120 were 10 per cent. Only 8.7 per cent of the flats had more than 120 square metres. This is not too unsatisfactory.

Considering that 91 per cent of Venetian flats have kitchens counted as rooms, the proportion of one-room flats in Venice is much below the national average, *i.e.* 8.7 per cent; the same applies to the proportion of two-room flats; while the proportion of flats with three or more rooms is larger in Venice than in Italy as a whole.

Of the premises lacking all sanitation, 43.5 per cent have the WC outside the building. However, that category is composed almost exclusively of housing on the island of Burano.

As to flats equipped with bathrooms, only 6.4 per cent have more than one. Most of the housing described as insanitary (80.2 per cent of such housing) is in the rented category; 62.8 per cent of it is in the controlled-rent group.

Water, electricity and heat

The survey showed that 1.6 per cent of the housing units have no running water. On Burano, more than a third of the houses are not connected to the mains. Although few houses lack both electricity and gas, 10.2 per cent of the total have electricity only. Burano has no gas mains; some houses in the Castello district and on the Giudecca also have no gas.

The kind of housing in the historic centre of Venice does not lend itself ideally to the installation of central heating or even, in many cases, of individual central heating arrangements. Only 28.8 per cent of housing has efficient heating. Even in the 23.6 per cent where all the rooms are heated by stoves or equivalent means, the standard is below that of the mainland. The percentage of housing without heating or inadequate heat is 47.6 per cent, representing more than 18,700 dwellings.

The layout of central Venice, with its labyrinth of very narrow streets, the vamous *calli* (alley-ways), has the disadvantage of restricting the light in a number of houses: in winter, 19.3 per cent of houses have less than two hours' daylight in twenty-four hours, while 45.3 have two to four hours.

This means that in winter a great many dwellings have to be lit by artificial light for a large part of the day: 13.5 per cent of houses have to use electric light in nearly all rooms for many hours a day; while another 24.4 per cent have some rooms which need artificial light for several hours a day.

Venice is, by its nature, damp unless special measures are taken to prevent it: in 15.5 per cent of dwellings there is damp due to salt and its hygroscopic effect; in 6.8 per cent this form of damp is not very marked; 22.2 per cent suffer from damp due to faulty roofs or walls; 55 per cent show no signs of damp. The proportion of housing affected by damp is higher in the controlled rent category than in the other categories.

State of repair

However, the number of buildings in unsafe condition is very small, between 0.3 per cent (housing units) and 0.8 per cent (carrying elements). There are of course dilapidated houses in urgent need of

169

Abandoned convent of S. Codomo on the Isle of Guudecca used as local housing

attention, and, too, a proportion in good condition. But more than 31 per cent of Venetian houses are in need of extensive repairs.

Of the flats in good condition 1.1 per cent are located in buildings which are in very bad condition, and 40 per cent in buildings which are shabby.

The urgency of repairs
Of premises let at controlled rents, more than 40 per cent are unsatisfactory. Of those let at an uncontrolled rent, more than 33 per cent are unsatisfactory. The largest proportion of dilapidated flats (85 per cent) is composed of those measuring less than 80 square metres. The proportion of good quality flats rises with an increase in size.

To sum up Venetian housing, out of a total of 39,400 dwellings, 12,400 are in need of major repairs, 2,400 of them in urgent need. Of the 12,400 units, approximately 6,200 have a surface area of less than 60 square metres, 5,500 are in the controlled rent category.

After the fall of the Republic of Venice in 1797, the measures taken to relieve the social and economic depression of the city, where many famous buildings were being destroyed, included: first, setting up industries in the historic centre (these proved to be an utter failure); and secondly, establishing cheap housing in outlying areas, together with transport and services.

The general policy, during the eighteenth and early nineteenth centuries, was to build cheap housing either to replace old buildings or in vacant areas. Virtually nothing was done in the way of renovation. This is confirmed by the replies given to questions relating to the date of the buildings in which the flats are located. It was found that 57.5 per cent of the flats were in buildings that dated from 1860 or before. From then to 1920, the buildings which contained 22.8 per cent of the flats were erected. Only 11.7 per cent of the flats were in buildings of the period 1920 to 1945, while 8 per cent were in buildings built after 1945.

In 1846 the railway bridge across the lagoon between Santa Lucia and Mestre was constructed; 1891 was the year of the *Piano Regolatore* providing for urban development mainly by building on vacant spaces.

Many existing residential buildings were erected before 1860. The survey showed that 36.9 per cent of the dwelling units were in pre-1860 buildings of a modest character. In really ancient buildings were 5.4 per cent. Handsome old residential buildings, not ancient, contained 7.1 per cent. Only 2.6 per cent of the dwelling units were in historic buildings.

Four per cent were in former convents and storehouses and other

171

structures not intended for living, while 10.3 per cent were in handsome and well-constructed modern buildings. The second largest proportion of dwellings, 29.9 per cent, were in modern residential buildings which were of poor quality.

As regards the town planning aspect of Venice, data were assembled on other features indicative of the standard of Venetian housing, such as the approach (other than by canal). The peculiar layout of the historic centre of Venice, with its maze of narrow streets, many of them ending in a *cul-de-sac,* offers many possibilities. Within six categories, there are main types of house: those approached from a series of narrow alleys *(calli)*; from a narrow street opening off a wide one and either leading on elsewhere or coming to a dead end; and from a wide street or a square. Classifying these three types of approach as mediocre, satisfactory and good respectively, the following figures were obtained: 17.6 per cent of the houses have a mediocre approach by land; 29.7 per cent of the houses have a satisfactory approach; 52.7 of the houses have a good approach.

The flooding of flats
A more important point is to discover how many of the houses are affected by what is known as 'high water' *(aqua alta),* a phenomenon which has become increasingly common in recent years. 'High water' is not merely a high tide; it is the result of a normal, or virtually normal tide, occuring when the sea itself has already risen to an abnormal level. This is described in 'Report of Venice' drawn up by Unesco in 1969.

In 34.9 per cent of the flats flooding is frequent at ground floor level; in 33.8 per cent flooding is rare; in 22.6 per cent flooding occurs only very exceptionally; in 8.7 per cent flooding has never occurred.

Ordinary high tides should be taken to mean those when the water rises to less than a metre above normal; unusually high ones, when the water rises to between a metre and 110 centimetres above normal level; and exceptional ones, when the water rises to more than 110 centimetres above normal.

The exceptional tide of 4th November 1966, when the water reached a level of 194 centimetres, was not counted in the survey. Thus it will be seen that 'high water', even in a 'normal' form occurring regularly at least several days in the year, affects a considerable number of Venetian houses.

There is the question of the distance of buildings from the nearest public transport, elementary schools and kindergartens. Over 80 per cent are within ten minutes of these facilities, which be regarded as satisfactory.

Unoccupied dwellings constitute 4 per cent of the total, slightly below the average for the province. The proportion of unoccupied

172

flats is much larger in the small-area groups. The percentage of small flats unoccupied because they are either unlet or declared uninhabitable is noticeably high.

Unoccupied flats declared unfit for habitation by the owners themselves proved particularly unsatisfactory in regard to conveniences, heating systems and signs of damp. In view both of their state of repair and date of construction, renovation would obviously be very costly, even though most are small. For those in process of renovation, the situation may be said to be satisfactory.

In the case of unlet flats, almost all of which are in pre-1920 buildings, their defects concern mainly the heating system which, in 73.1 per cent, is either unsatisfactory or mediocre.

Flats situated either at street level or below street level *(pianterreni)* have always been a feature of Venetian housing. It is they which suffer most from 'high water'; besides which they lack both air and sun, and are permanently damp.

In 1910, according to the survey published by R. Vivante, there were 2,465 ground-floor dwellings in the historic centre of Venice (10.5 per cent of the total), occupied by 12,086 persons, constituting 8.9 per cent of the Venetian population. These ground-floor flats were most common in the Castello and Cannaregio districts and on the Giudecca; and 1,967 (80 per cent) were classified as unfit for habitation. These ground-floor premises had previously been either storehouses or entrance halls giving access to the floors above.

Another survey made in 1935, for the purpose of verifying the number of dwellings which were uninhabitable, showed 1,245 ground-floor flats classed as uninhabitable, *i.e.* fewer than in 1910, while the total number was about 2,000; and showed that these flats were occupied by 6,568 persons. A third survey, made in 1948, gave 1,769 ground-floor flats unfit for habitation, occupied by 9,048 people, a situation very close to that for 1910 (even as regards the total number of ground-floor premises).

This was because building ceased during and after World War II, and also because of the exceptional influx of population during that period, composed partly of refugees from Istria and Dalmatia, which resulted in the re-occupation of many ground-floor premises classed as uninhabitable and the taking over of many storehouses for living in.

The Town Planning Department of the Commune of Venice, in 1957 made a sample survey of housing in the historic centre. This showed an even larger number of ground-floor flats: 11.7 per cent of the total housing, or more than 4,100 units, located mainly in the Castello and Cannaregio districts and on the Giudecca.

Of these, 33.8 per cent were classified as unfit for habitation (because they lacked the requisite sanitation, were located in buildings designed for other purposes, or were in a bad or very bad state of repair); and 43.5 per cent were classified as overcrowded (more than two persons per room). It was stated, further, that *all* flats below the first floor should, generally speaking, be classed as unfit for habitation!

Thus, though several studies have been made of the problem of ground-floor flats, they have not been followed by practical measures to remedy the situation. Indeed, it is shown that ground-floor premises constitute 11.8 per cent of the total housing. In the historic centre of Venice, the number of ground-floor dwellings exceeds 4,600 — over 2,000 more than in 1910. This indicates that the assumption has always been, when building in Venice, that the ground floor will be used for living in. At all events 92.5 per cent of these flats (slightly below 4,300 units) are occupied by some 13,500 persons (exactly 11 per cent of the Venetian population, not counting those sharing flats). Of the rented ground-floor flats, the largest proportion are privately owned; in the controlled rent category, the proportion owned by the public authorities is slightly higher than for housing as a whole. Public authorities owned 34 per cent of these ground-floor flats under controlled rent, while owning 22.7 per cent of housing as a whole. Also publicly owned were 6.4 per cent at uncontrolled rent. Private ownership had 65.5 per cent of these controlled-rent flats and 93.6 per cent of the uncontrolled.

About two thirds of ground-floor flats were found unsuitable for habitation; practically all of them should be used for other purposes.

Study of Venetians' employment

Of the 3,936 flats covered by the survey, 3,776 were occupied by 12,251 persons, representing slightly less than 10 per cent of the population of Venice. The employed numbered 31.3 per cent; the unemployed 1.3 per cent; while 1.6 per cent were waiting to take up their first job. The remaining 65.8 per cent were housewives, pensioners, students, etc.

Outstanding is the low rate of unemployment, below that considered normal in developed economic systems. But what is most striking about the position in the historic centre of Venice is that only 34.2 per cent of the people normally work in jobs.

This reduction in the size of the active population in relation to the whole is a phenomenon also observed at the regional and national level (the figures for 1969 were 37.5 per cent and 36.7 per cent respectively); and special studies have been made on the subject. The explanations of a fall in the labour force include demographic factors (ageing of the population, increased number of married women); social factors (extension of schooling, extension of the pension system, etc.); and structural factors.

In the case of the historic centre of Venice, the fact that so small a percentage of the population works is due directly to demographic factors which, in their turn, are closely linked with the steady decline of the Venetian population. This is the result of a drop in the rate of natural increase and of the fact that emigration has exceeded immigration: the average age has risen in consequence from 34.5 in 1951 and 37.8 in 1961 to 40 in 1969.

This change in average age has brought about a profound change in the composition of the Venetian population: fewer young people and children, and increasing number of middle-aged who, as time passes, will swell the ranks of the aged: such changes are obviously important, economically as well as demographically, and influence the production and distribution of goods, and mentality, tastes and the way of life.

A young population is more dynamic, more adaptable and has a greater working capacity. The ageing of the population is a main cause of low productivity, and of the large number inactive to every active member of the population (as pointed out by *Observatorio Economico*). The population movement has also changed the social structure, because it has mainly affected people in certain income brackets.

The occupations of people of the historic centre of Venice represent a variance in proportion with those of Italy in general: managerial, in Venice, 1.9 per cent, compared with 0.9 per cent in Italy; liberal professions, 3.7 per cent, compared with 0.8 per cent; independent workers, 19.1 per cent, compared with 30.7 per cent; white-collar workers, 27.4 per cent compared with 11.8 per cent; manual, 47.9 per cent compared with 55.8 per cent. The implications of the employment situation in the historic centre are of considerable importance. First, the exodus from Venice is due less to lack of employment than to other causes and, in particular, housing. People in the middle and lower-middle income brackets (*i.e.* independent and white-collar workers) tend to live elsewhere while continuing to work in Venice. Those in the higher income brackets, unlike manual workers, stay. Secondly, the social structure is very lop-sided, because the city does not offer a sufficient variety of basic employment. The result of this is that Venice gives the impression of being culturally 'depressed', because the various social strata of the population are so isolated that cultural contact between them is difficult.

The questionnaire for the survey included questions to ascertain the desires of occupants. People were asked whether they intended to move out of their current lodgings and if so, for what reasons. It was found that 32.6 per cent wanted to move, the majority of them because of the lack of modern conveniences. This affects 36.2 per cent of the total housing. Of those in managerial occupations 0.7 per cent wanted to move; in liberal professions, 1.2 per cent; in independent work, 13.1 per cent; white collar workers, 22.9 per cent; manual workers, 62.1 per cent. It is always the people in the less-paid occupations who wish to move out of the lodgings. However, the vast majority (85.7 per cent) said that they wished to continue living in the historic centre of Venice. Over half would continue to live in Venice if they could find flats there of the same standard and at the same rent as elsewhere.

Of the families interviewed 71.8 per cent were Venetian by origin; 24.6 per cent had immigrated before 1951. It is thus understandable that most should want to remain in Venice. The fact that there is an exodus is further confirmation that it is the housing conditions which force them to leave. Of the people who mean to leave their lodgings, 61.3 per cent intend to rent, 34.3 per cent to buy (outright or by deferred payment); 4.4 per cent have not yet made up their minds. Lastly, as regards the rent they could pay for a satisfactory, well-planned flat, 87.3 per cent replied – at that time – less than 30,000 lires a month, 11.9 per cent between 30,000 and 50,000 and the rest (barely 0.8 per cent) – more than 50,000.

Implications of the Study

One of the most important events in the life of Venice – after it lost its dominant economic, political and social role during the early twentieth century – was the creation of the industrial zone and port of the Marghera on the western shores of the lagoon. It was thought that the establishment of petrochemical and other industries would make up for the declining fortunes of traditional arts and crafts and that this would stimulate a new life for the Venetians.

Much of the shallows were filled, a deep water port was dredged, ship canals were built, and plants erected. However, filling the shallows resulted in increased danger from high water: the needs of industry for fresh water resulted in sinking artesian wells which contributed to the lowering of the water table, and the resultant compression of the subsoil to overall subsidence. New housing developments in the Mestre, adjacent to the Marghera, attract the inhabitants of the old city and contribute to the loss of its population.

The great flood of the 3rd and 4th November 1966 dramatised to the world the plight of Venice. This study is one of many others which have since taken place (under contract to Unesco) concurrently to diagnose the different, closely inter-related ills of one of the most important and beautiful historic cities in the world. On the basis of these studies, and the world-wide interest and concern in the future of the city, a special law was drafted and adopted by the Italian Parliament on 13th April 1973, to raise through loans 300 billion lire (about US $510 million) for work to be carried out to ensure the safeguarding of Venice. The law foresees *a)* the building of gates at the outlets of the ship canals leading to the lagoon to protect it against high water; *b)* combatting and reducing atmospheric and other types of pollution; *c)* installing aqueducts and closing off artesian wells; *d)* building a new sewage system for the discharge of sewage; and *e)* restoring the monuments and works of art of the city. Finally, 4 billion lire to improve housing is foreseen for the municipalities of Venice and Chioggia.

APPENDIX I: SUMMARY OF UNESCO MISSIONS IN THE CONSERVATION OF CULTURAL PROPERTY

Unesco has the privilege of being able to provide expert and disinterested advice and help to countries all over the world which are becoming increasingly conscious of their often neglected treasures and of their duty to safeguard them, not only for themselves, but for mankind.

Afghanistan — Several Unesco missions between 1969 and 1974 to study cultural tourist possibilities in Bamiyan Valley, northern Afghanistan, and the historic city of Herat.

Algeria — Major monument restoration programme (launched 1963) now expanded by excavation of Roman remains at Tipasa, conservation of the Casbah in Algiers, the Honain ramparts, the port of Cap Matifou, rock paintings in southern Algeria, and the Galca des Beni Hammad. Programme for international exchange of cultural property in preparation; plan for restoration laboratory in Algiers. Various Unesco missions 1966–73.

Andean Route — Five countries (Bolivia, Chile, Colombia, Ecuador, Peru) participating in large-scale regional project to preserve the cultural heritage of the Andean Region. Several Unesco missions since 1970.

Bolivia — Five-year plan for cultural sites, including archaeological remains of Tiahuanaco; survey of tourist resources in Altiplano areas, and of baroque churches in La Paz, Oruro, Potosi, Cochabamba. Unesco missions 1966 and 1973.

Brazil — A broad cultural resources programme planned in co-operation with Brazilian specialists as part of the nation-wide economic development plan; special attention to sites at Salvador de Bahia, Ouro Preto, Parati, Alcantara, Olinda. Unesco missions 1966, 1967, 1968–71. Three missions in 1972.

Bulgaria — Conservation of murals in Thracian tomb at Kazanluk. Restoration of murals in churches of the Forty Martyrs, Sveta Peta (Sofia) and Bojana. Unesco mission 1966.

Cambodia — Safeguarding the archaeological sites near Angkor Wat.

Unesco missions 1968 and 1969.

Cameroon — Restoration programme for Foumban Palace and inventory of works of art in palaces and houses of chieftains. Unesco mission 1968.

Colombia — Plans for restoration at Cartagena de Indias, a large port on the Caribbean founded in 1533, which still has many early monuments — ramparts, palaces, churches, monasteries. Pre-Hispanic sites being considered in connection with cultural tourist development include San Agustin. Four missions in 1972.

Cyprus — Inventory and conservation programme for monuments and sites, gothic churches, and mosques. Plan to restore 800 square metres of Roman mosaics at Kato Paphos. Restoration of Selimiye Mosque (St Sophia Gothic Cathedral). Various Unesco missions 1966—73. Inventory of monuments to be restored completed April 1972.

Czechoslovakia — Mission in connection with a project to transfer the Gothic church at Most from its present unsatisfactory site.

Dahomey — Programme for conservation and restoration of royal palaces at Abomey. Unesco missions 1965 and 1968.

Dominican Republic — Plan to conserve historic monuments and sites, some dating from arrival of Europeans in America. Unesco mission 1968.

Chile — Plan for making Easter Island into a vast museum of pre-historic Polynesian civilisation and restoring the colossal statues, drawn up in 1966 and 1968 by Unesco archaeological and ethnological mission in co-operation with Chilean archaeologists. Restoration of the Church of San Francisco in Santiago and creation of a museum. Various missions 1969—72.

El Salvador — Restoration of pre-Mayan sites. Missions in 1972 and 1974.

Ethiopia — National programme for historic monuments and sites. Creation of library of microfilms of ancient manuscripts. New regulations governing the export of cultural property. Restoration started in Gondar. Projects for Axum and Lake Tana. Unesco missions 1971—74.

Greece — Photogrammetry survey of the stability of the Parthenon. Unesco mission 1970—71.

Guatemala – Plans for restoration of Tikal, a famous Maya site.

Haiti – Unesco mission in 1971 to advise the Government on the preparation of an inventory and on restoration procedures.

Honduras – Restoration of the Maya site of Copan. Unesco missions, in 1972 and 1974.

India – Programme for the conservation of monuments and temples in southern India, including the temples of Srirangam, near Madras, and Rameswaram at the southern tip of India. Missions to help in planning cultural tourism in Northern India, 1966–71.

Indonesia – Urgent restoration programme, partially financed through international voluntary contributions, to save the temple of Borobudur and its 1,400 bas-reliefs. Plans to create tourist circuit in Central Java after restoration of other sites, including Prambanan, Sewu and Plaøsan. Various Unesco missions since 1968.

Iran – Large-scale programme for tourist development. The 80 million dollars allocated in the national budget (1968–73) for highways, hotels, and so on includes 4 million dollars for selected sites and monuments in four priority areas: 1) Between Teheran and Mount Ararat (outstanding sites, Armenian medieval churches, Mongol monuments, the ancient capital of Quazvin, the mausoleums of Soltarieln and Ardebil); 2) Teheran and surroundings (museums, palaces, Mongol shrines, Sassanian fire temple); 3) Isfahan, city monument and gem of Islamic civilisation; 4) Sharaz area, cradle of ancient Persia, and many sites (including Persepolis and Firouzabad). Some forty Unesco missions between 1966 and 1972.

Iraq – Art conservation laboratory opened in Baghdad; soil surveys of ancient sites; plan for conservation of monuments. Unesco missions 1966 and 1968.

Italy – International campaign for Florence and Venice launched by Unesco following floods of 4th November 1966. Two special 'painting hospitals' will continue operations in Florence for several years. Laboratories supplied with Unesco equipment. Help in restoration of Tuscany archives. Systematic survey, with Unesco aid, into the state of preservation of monuments and works of art in Venice.

Jamaica – On 7th June 1692, Port Royal, an important trading centre in the New World, was obliterated by an earthquake and tidal wave.

180

Recent underwater archaeology has brought to light many objects of great historic and artistic value. In 1967, a Unesco mission helped Jamaican authorities organise a programme for the conservation of underwater finds. Other missions advised on cultural tourism and the conservation of sites and monuments.

Latin American Regional Project — An inter-governmental conference held in Asunción, Paraguay, in May 1972 approved a project for the preservation of the former Jesuit missions in the *Cone Sur* (Brazil, Argentina, Paraguay, Uruguay and Chile). Unesco will provide technical assistance.

Libya — Archaeological research programme, including excavations of Islamic sites; conservation service set up; team of archaeologists trained to supervise excavations. Unesco mission 1964–65. Unesco mission in 1972 in connection with restoration of bronze objects.

Malta — Conservation programme for the Vilhena Palace at M'dina, the Gran Castello in Gozo, the Fort of St Angelo at Valletta, and for prehistoric, Phoenician and Roman sites. Plan for the reorganisation of the National Archaeological Museum. Three Unesco missions 1965 to 1967.

Mexico — Conservation of the frescoes in the Maya temple at Bonampak. Latin American centre for conservation of cultural property set up near Mexico City by Mexican Government and Unesco. Six Unesco specialists teach techniques for restoring art works of Pre-Colombian and later periods. Training and refresher courses for museum and monument conservators from all parts of Latin America. Various Unesco missions since 1966.

Mongolia — Unesco missions 1971–74 in connection with the preservation of Buddhist temples.

Nepal — Plans for the conservation of richly carved monuments at Kathmandu, Patan, Bhaktapur and Kirtipur; inventory of major historic buildings, in co-operation with Nepalese authorities and the United Nations; creation of a restoration laboratory. Unesco missions in 1970–74.

Panama — Plans for the preservation of Portobello and Panama la Antigua.

Pakistan — Restoration programme linked with plans for tourist

development at Karachi, Lahore and Dacca. Plans to save
Moenjodaro, one of the most ancient sites yet found anywhere in
the world. Some ten Unesco missions between 1966–74. International
Campaign to save Moenjodaro launched in 1974.

Peru – Large-scale tourist development project for the Cuzco-Machu
Picchu- area, cradle of the Inca Empire. Plans for a new National
Museum of Archaeology, Ethnology and History near Lima.
Restoration of historic monuments in the area affected by the
earthquake of May 1970. Restoration of the Santa Catalina
Monastery. Numerous missions since 1965.

Sri Lanka – Two missions in 1971 and 1972 to study cultural tourism
possibilities at the historic cities of Anuradhapura, Pollonaruwa and
Kandy, with two other missions (1970 and 1972) in connection with
the preservation of frescoes in these areas.

Sudan – Archaeological exploration of sites in Nile Valley between
Gemai and the Third Cataract, in southern part of area to be flooded
by Aswan High Dam. Various missions 1959 to 1970.

Syria – Programme of conservation and research for thirty-four
ancient sites (mausoleums, citadels, minarets) in areas of Upper
Euphrates to be flooded by waters of new dam near Tabqa.
Photogrammetric and topographical records made; plans for removal
of monuments in area to be inundated. Conservation laboratory
opened in National Museum, Damascus. Restoration of ancient city of
Bosra (Roman monuments, citadel, twelfth century mosque). Five
Unesco missions 1967–68.

Thailand – Studies made of best techniques for conserving temples
(Bangkok, Ayuthia, Phnom Rung, Thonburi, Sukhotai, Lampang)
and murals damaged by humidity. Unesco missions 1967 and 1974.

Tunisia – Two major restoration programmes: sites and monuments
in the Tunis-Carthage area; and the extensive Roman remains at
Bulla Regia. Various Unesco missions 1967–73. International
archaeological salvage programme launched for Carthage.

Turkey – Programme combining preservation and restoration of art
treasures and historic monuments with tourist development
(Cappadocia, Pamphylia, coastal regions of Izmir and Antalaya). Several
Unesco missions since 1965.

United Arab Republic – Saving of Nubian monuments in Egypt and Sudan under the Unesco international campaign, including removal of the temples of Abu Simbel to a new site; temples of Philae will similarly be dismantled and rebuilt nearby, beyond the reach of the Nile. Plan to protect the site of the Pyramids. Various Unesco missions.

Yugoslavia – Laboratory equipment provided for the National Museum in Belgrade, and Zagreb Museum; Unesco fellowships to help train specialists for conservation and restoration of manuscripts, books and ancient art objects.

APPENDIX II   NOTES ON CONTRIBUTORS

Francine Dominique Champault – Ph.D., University of Paris, 1957. Specialised in Ethnology. Missions for the Musée de l'Homme in North Africa and for Unesco in Tunisia and Madagascar. Research Associate, Centre National de la Recherche Scientifique since 1949; in charge of the Department of North African and Near Eastern Cultures, Musée de l'Homme, Paris, since 1959.

Hiroshi Daifuku – B.A., University of Hawaii (1942); Ph.D., Harvard University (1951); Instructor, Cultural Anthropology, University of Wisconsin (1949-52); Assistant Curator, State Historical Society Museum, Madison, Wisconsin (1952-53); Unesco, Programme Specialist, Development of Museums (1954-62). Preservation of Cultural Property (1962-66); Chief, Monuments and Sites Division (1967–).

Jellal El Kafi – Engineer. Landscape architect (Government diploma). Town planning diploma, Institut d'Urbanisme de l'Université de Paris. Town Planner, Tunis municipality. Director of the town planning workshop of the Association for the Safeguarding of the Medina. Author of *Croissance Urbaine et Modèles de Croissance: La Ville de Tunis 1881-1970* and 'Carthage must not be destroyed' *(Unesco Courier)*.

Hans Foramitti – Graduated in architecture, Technical University of Vienna (1952); doctorate (1958); Assistant, History of Architecture, Higher Technical College, Vienna (1953-54); Departmental Director (1955-57); Librarian (1957-61); Curator, Department of Architecture, Federal Service for Historic Monuments, Austria (1961–); Director, Photogrammetry Department and Commissioner-General for the Application of The Hague Convention in Austria.

Piero Gazzola – Doctorate in Architecture, Milan Polytechnic (1932); D. ès L., University of Milan (1934); Deputy Architect, Ministry of Education (1935-50); Superintendent for Monuments and Galleries (1950-55); Programme Specialist Unesco (1953-54); Inspector, Ministry of Public Education (1955-74); Italian Representative on the Council of the Rome Centre (1959–); President, International Council of Monuments and Sites (1965–).

Teiji Itoh – Graduated in Architecture, University of Tokyo (1945);

Assistant to Professor Sekino, University of Tokyo (1947-50) and research (1950-65); Visiting Professor of Architecture, University of Washington (1963-65); Professor of Architecture, Kogakuin University (1972).

Koji Nishikawa – M.E., University of Kyoto (1956), Doctorate (1968); Assistant Professor of Architecture, Kyoto University (1968–); worked on architectural and archaeological survey of ancient monuments in Gandhara 1960, 1962, 1963, 1965, 1968; architectural survey of Buddhist monuments in Mongolia on behalf of Unesco, 1971.

Maximilian Piperek – University studies in psychology, biology, education. Doctorate in letters. Taught in Vienna (1932-45); Museum Director, Salzburg (1945-48); Research in labour and vocational guidance questions, Social Affairs Ministry (1945-72); Private practice in psychology; university lecturer in psychology in Vienna and Zurich. President, Austrian Society of Psychology; member, Council of Austrian Mental Health Society, scientific adviser to Federal Ministry for Health and the Protection of the Environment.

Mario Rinaldo – Graduated in Economics, University of Venice (1967); Director of Research, Venice Chamber of Commerce (1958-62); Director, *Osservatorio Economico* (1962-71); Town Planning Consultant, Venice (1969); Director of Research Veneto Regional Union of Chambers of Commerce (1968-71); Technical Director for Veneto Region, 1972.

Graeme Shankland – M.A. (Architecture), Diploma in Town Planning, Associate of the Royal Institute of British Architects, Fellow of the Royal Town Planning Institute, RIBA Distinction in Town Planning. Planning Division, London County Council, 1962; Planning consultant to the City Council of Liverpool, 1962. Supervised major town planning projects and prepared regional studies in: Britain, Dominica, France, Jamaica, Malaysia, Santa Lucia, and Yugoslavia; detailed plans for residential areas in the United Kingdom, New York City, Brazil and Peru.

M.F. Siroux – Studies at Ecole Nationale Supérieure des Beaux Arts, Paris. Graduated in architecture (1934); Architect to Mission Archéologique Française (Musée du Louvre) (1933-34); Chief Architect to Iranian Ministry of Architecture (1935); Professor, Teheran University (1935-45), and consultant to Historic Monuments Service; Architect for State Public works in Morocco, (1948-58), Iran (1958-63), France (1965–); missions to Iran for Unesco (1968, 1970, 1972).

185

François Sorlin – Doctorate, University of Lille (1930); Diploma History of Art, University of Paris (1932); Inspector of Historical Monuments (1936); French Buildings Service (1949-59); Inspector-General Historical Monuments (1960–); Professor, Centre for Conservation of Historical Monuments, Paris (1960-71) and International Centre for the Conservation of Cultural Property, Rome (1966-71).

Christopher Tunnard – Visiting Lecturer, Harvard University Graduate School of Design (1939-42); Wheelwright Travelling Fellow in Architecture, Harvard (1943-4); Director of Planning Studies, Yale University (1946–); Professor of City Planning, Yale University (1961–); Doctor of Fine Arts (Hon.), Union College (1966); Member, United States Advisory Council on Historic Preservation (1966-8); Member United States National Committee for ICOMOS (1968–); Doctor at Laws (Hon.), University of Victoria, Canada (1970).